CALLED TO BE

H O L Y

CALLED TO BE
HOLY

ARCHBISHOP TIMOTHY M. DOLAN

Our Sunday Visitor Publishing
Our Sunday Visitor, Inc.
Huntington, Indiana 46750

Our Sunday Visitor Publishing Division
Our Sunday Visitor, Inc.
200 Noll Plaza
Huntington, IN 46750

ISBN: 1-59276-072-4 (Inventory No. T123)
LCCN: 2004117317

Cover design by Monica Haneline
Cover photo is "The Universal Call to Holiness," Basilica of the National Shrine of the Immaculate Conception, Washington, D.C.
Interior design by Sherri L. Hoffman

PRINTED IN THE UNITED STATES OF AMERICA

To Lisa, Chris, Kelly, and Shannon,
who taught me a lot about grace, faith, and holiness.

Contents

Foreword

*Y*ou can't miss it. It covers the south wall of the Great Main Church of the Basilica of the National Shrine of the Immaculate Conception in Washington, D.C. It is called "The Universal Call to Holiness." It depicts men and women, children to senior citizens, rich and poor, black, white, red, brown, and yellow, farmers, factory laborers, business executives, married couples and single, all striving for a deeper union with Jesus.

It is a catechetical tool for one of the most poignant teachings of the Second Vatican Council: that the summons to sanctity is at the core of Christian discipleship, an imperative for every baptized person. It is indeed a "universal call to holiness." The challenge to virtue, sanctity, and perfection is not limited to monks and nuns, but is a charge to *all*.

It took an ecumenical council to remind us that, but it is hardly a new teaching. It is so clear in the preaching of Jesus. It was a refrain in great saints such as Francis de Sales, Thérèse of Liseiux, and Jose Maria Escriva.

And it is clear in this little book. The chapters herein were originally conferences I gave to priests and seminarians while rector of the North American College in Rome, published by Our Sunday Visitor as *Priests for the Third Millennium*. Some readers graciously observed that a lot of the book would be appropriate for lay people as well.

They are right! That's what we call the "universal call to holiness!"

✠ Timothy M. Dolan, Archbishop of Milwaukee
Feast of the Transfiguration, 2004

The next day again John was standing with two of his disciples; and he looked at Jesus as he walked, and said, "Behold, the Lamb of God!" The two disciples heard him say this, and they followed Jesus. Jesus turned, and saw them following, and said to them, "What do you seek?" And they said to him, "Rabbi" (which means Teacher), "where are you staying?" He said to them, "Come and see." They came and saw where he was staying; and they stayed with him.

— Jn. 1: 35–39

CHAPTER 1

———✠———

Being Good Stewards
with the Gifts of the Holy Spirit

The Only Reason We Exist

*I*t is with the account from the Gospel of St. John of the Master's invitation —"Come and see" — and of the disciples' acceptance —"…so they went and saw where he lived, and stayed with him…" that I wish to begin because, of course, Jesus Christ is the only real reason we exist. He is the One who calls and the One who empowers us to respond to His call; He is the end for which we strive; He is the means to that end; without Him, we can do nothing; with Him, nothing is impossible. Everything we embark upon is for, with, through, and because of Jesus Christ.

As St. Paul wrote to the Colossians:

> He is the image of the invisible God, the first-born of all creation; for in him all things were created, in heaven and on earth, visible and invisible, whether thrones or dominions or principalities or authorities — all things were created through him and for him. He is before all things, and in him all things hold together. He is the head of the body, the church; he is the beginning, the first-born from the dead, that in everything he might be pre-eminent. For in him all the fulness of God was pleased to

dwell, and through him to reconcile to himself all things, whether on earth or in heaven, making peace by the blood of his cross.

— COL. 1:15–20

Here is the key to our spiritual growth: a faithful, personal, loving relationship with Jesus. As theologian Karl Rahner writes, *holiness* is "participation in the intimate union between Father and Son, led by the Spirit." Jesus Christ is the *way* to accomplish this through the *truth* He teaches, and the *life* He imparts. Listen to these poetic words of Pope Paul VI:

Jesus is Christ, the Son of the Living God. Because of Him we come to know the God we cannot see. He is the firstborn of all creation, in Him all things find their being. Our teacher and redeemer, He was born for us, died for us, and for us rose from the dead.

All things converge in Christ. A man of sorrow and hope, He knows us and loves us. As our friend, He stays with us throughout our lives; at the end of time He will come to be our judge; but we also know that He will be the complete fulfillment of our lives and our great happiness for all eternity.

I can never cease to speak of Christ. He is the way, the truth, and the life. He is our bread, our living water, who allays our hunger and satisfies our thirst. He is our shepherd, our leader, our ideal, our comforter, and our brother.

Jesus Christ is the beginning and the end, the alpha and the omega, Lord of the universe, the great hidden key to human history and the part we play in it. He is the mediator between heaven and earth, true God and true Man.

To know Jesus, to hear Jesus, to love Jesus, to trust Jesus, to obey Jesus, to share His life in the deepest fiber of our being, and then to serve Him — this is our goal. Beware, though. As Cardinal William Baum once preached, "The danger . . . is to know about Jesus without knowing Him, to talk about Jesus but not to Him, to listen to experts speak of Him without letting Him speak about Himself. A deep, personal, intimate relationship with Jesus Christ is the foundation of holiness!"

"Seek ye first the kingdom of God!" exhorts Our Lord. The primacy of the spiritual! Stewardship of the supernatural gifts of grace, faith, mercy, prayer, sacraments, and vocation that the Lord gives us! Stewardship, of course, means a responsible care for the gifts entrusted to us.

When I was rector at the Pontifical North American College in Rome, Italy, its spiritual enterprise was, and still is, *Christological* and *ecclesial*, to grow in love for and to understand what the Church is, what she asks, and what she needs from the men who detect a call to lead her in this millennium. When we ponder what the Church needs from her priests, and from her people as well, one word towers above all the rest: holiness. The Church needs holy priests and a holy laity. As Pope John Paul II's apostolic exhortation on the formation of priests, *Pastores Dabo Vobis,* so clearly states:

> The priest must be a man of God, the one who belongs to God and makes people think of God. . . . Christians expect to find in the priest. . . . a man who will help them turn to God . . . and so the priest must have a deep intimacy with the Lord. Those who are preparing for the priesthood should realize that their whole priestly life will have value, inasmuch as they are able to give themselves to Christ, and, through Christ, to the Father.

The laity, like priests, aspire to give Christ to others, but they can't give Him unless they've got him! That is holiness. Pope Paul VI says it well in his apostolic exhortation *Evangelii Nuntiandi:* "Before we evangelize, we must be evangelized."

How do we grow in holiness? How? That, of course, is our spiritual program, isn't it, the stewardship of the spirit, "the regimen of the soul bringing about the reign of God," to quote servant of the poor Charles de Foucauld. I propose to you a spiritual regimen, a stewardship of the spirit coming not from me, but from centuries of practice and learning.

I. Daily Prayer

Patient, persevering, persistent prayer, every day, is number one. Here I am not speaking of the Mass — such as the Eucharist — but of silent, personal, private prayer, a daily period of quiet communion with the Lord, conscious of His presence, accepting His love, and returning it with praise, petition, and thanksgiving. Call it what you want—meditation, centering, contemplation — I've never seen it better described than by the great Belgian Cardinal Desire Mercier, who wrote:

> Every day for some moments . . . close your eyes to the things of sense and your ears to the noises of the world, in order to enter into yourself. There, in the sanctity of your baptized soul, the temple of the Holy Spirit, say: "O Holy Spirit, beloved of my soul, I adore you. Enlighten me, guide me, strengthen me, console me. . . . Let me know your will." If you do this, your life will flow serenely, even in the midst of trials. This submission to the Holy Spirit is the secret of sanctity.

Daily prayer is the foundation of this sanctity . . . to nourish it, develop it, intensify it is the goal of a lifetime. Some do it beautifully early in the morning, some late at night; some come before the Blessed Sacrament, others in the privacy of their homes; some rely on Scripture, or devotions; some utilize the Holy Hour format — however, wherever, whenever, whatever — a daily period of private prayer is a must!

II. Daily Mass

I defer again to Pope John Paul in *Pastores Dabo Vobis*:

> To be utterly frank and clear, I would like to say once again: it is fitting that seminarians take part every day in the Eucharistic celebration, in such a way that they will take up as a rule of their priestly life this daily celebration. They should . . . consider this Eucharistic celebration as the essential moment of their day in which they take an active part, and at which they will never be satisfied with a merely habitual attendance.

From this daily Eucharistic meal will come, not only for the seminarians mentioned above, but for all who celebrate the Eucharist as the essential moment of their day, a reverential awe for the Real Presence of Christ in the Blessed Sacrament, and a desire to spend time before Him there in visits and prayer.

III. Daily Fidelity to the Liturgy of the Hours

This ancient prayer of the Church is mostly associated with those in Holy Orders, who have as their duty the daily recitation of the Breviary at fixed times throughout the day. It is also intended to be the prayer of the laity, who "are encouraged to recite the divine office, either with the priests, or among themselves, or even individually" (*Catechism of the Catholic Church*, no. 1175).

IV. Daily Spiritual Reading

Lectio divina, daily reverent meditation upon Sacred Scripture, is first and foremost, of course, but I also speak of daily spiritual reading of the enduring books of our Catholic tradition, as well as interest in the burgeoning contemporary literature on the interior life. Nor should we forget attention to the documents of the magisterium, the words of our Holy Father, the documents of the Apostolic See, the messages and pastorals of our own bishops, all vehicles of the Holy Spirit for fostering our growth in sanctity.

V. Spiritual Direction

An honest, trusting, fruitful, consistent relationship with a spiritual director is, in some ways, the linchpin of all the rest, for this is where integration and interiorization begin to take place. The danger we all face is a life of formalism, where we passively do things just to get by, not allowing the values of formation to sink in and become part of us. Spiritual direction can promote this interiorization, this integration.

VI. The Sacrament of Penance

Regular reliance upon the mercy of God abundant in the Sacrament of Penance should be a priority in our lives. While how often you approach this sacrament is a good topic to discuss with your spiritual director, at least once a month seems a solid tradition of the Church. That you approach confession regularly is a hallmark of sound spiritual stewardship. And, a practical help to make our regular confessions more fruitful would be a daily examination of conscience, praising God for our growth, asking for healing of the faults we admit.

VII. Growing in Virtue

A tireless effort for growth in virtue and turning away from sin should be the pattern of our daily lives. Obedient to the constant refrain of the Gospels, we are always in the process of conversion, repentance, dying to sin, self, and Satan, rising to new life in Christ. This is the "paschal mystery." In practice, this means growth in virtue and struggle with sin. Development in particular virtues is most appropriate:

A. Faith

I recently received a letter from someone critical of his own spiritual formation. He said that throughout his life he was often asked, "Are you happy?" "Are you maturing?" "Are you open?" Never once did anyone ask, "Do you believe in God?" One would like to think that we can take some things for granted, and that belief in God would be one of them, but his point was a good one — the utter necessity of faith. We grow in our rock-sure belief in God, His Son, His revelation, and we reject doubt, cynicism, pervasive relativism, and an aimless existence, which stems from a lack of faith.

B. Hope

Hope is the firm, joyful reliance on the utter dependability of God's promises, and a rejection of the despair, gloom, and discouragement we often face.

C. Charity

Charity is a burning love for God and His people, evident in patience, service, sharing, courtesy, generosity, and joy; and a battle against our dark side, from which emerges hate, selfishness, laziness, petty resentment, and just plain meanness.

D. Simplicity of life

Seeking to live plainly, justly, and gratefully, a life of simplicity is achieved by not succumbing to the accumulation and stinginess endemic to Western society. Luxurious living and displays of affluence can be a source of great scandal to those with whom we share our faith.

E. Chastity

The Church calls all to lead "a chaste life in keeping with their particular states in life" (*CCC*, no. 2348), a striving that is performed deliberately, maturely, happily, and for the sake of the Kingdom. It is a surrendering of all genital activity in thought, word, and deed, alone, or with others, hetero-or-homo, honestly confronting any inclinations, drives, or fantasies that threaten the wholesome, healthy, realistic purity mirrored by Jesus and expected by His Church of her people.

F. Obedience

Obedience is a childlike docility to the Lord and His call, an attentiveness to the Church and her commandments, which calls us to reject the smug demand for unbridled liberty so popular today.

G. Integrity

Integrity is the cultivation of truthfulness, honesty, and keeping one's word. It is also the avoidance of deceit, shame, hypocrisy, and the drug of denial, which keeps us from genuine spiritual growth. Cardinal Joseph Bernardin once recalled those dark days when he was unjustly accused of molesting a teenager.

He said, "At that moment, when all looked bleak, all the worldly honors I had — position, cardinalate, prestige, fame, Chicago — did not help one bit. In fact, they hurt my cause. All I had were two things to rely on: God's grace, and my personal integrity. They worked." Integrity is a constant growth in virtue and a struggle with sin, leading to an ongoing conversion of life.

VIII. Devotion to the Blessed Mother and the Saints

Our devotion to them is a sustaining dependence upon the "Communion of Saints," an awareness that we are members of a supernatural family not confined to the here and now, that we have the saints as examples and helpers, pre-eminently, especially our Blessed Mother. Thus, a wholesome devotion to her would be an essential part of our spiritual regimen.

IX. Holistic Formation, Allowing Spirituality to Permeate Our Lives

The spiritual life is not a tidy, isolated compartment of our existence! No, as the Holy Father says, "Spiritual formation is the core which unifies and gives life to our entire being." Thus, every element of our lives is part of the spiritual arena, and growth in holiness will entail wholehearted immersion in a spiritual regimen.

A major part of our spiritual stewardship is human and personal development in qualities such as reliability, courtesy, promptness, and the fostering of genuine friendships so essential for a fruitful life.

Academic rigor plays a part as well, through consistent study and research, ongoing reading, theological refinement, and the cultivation of good reading habits. Also, we should nurture a zeal toward our daily work and our duties in life, as well as a sensitivity to the demands of our state in life, being a real support for one another, just looking out for one another; a contribution through time, effort, and presence.

I once was in a parish discussion group that was to ponder "married life and family." The leader set the ground rules and said, "Let's only talk about our married and family life, nothing about our jobs." One of the men, who had a tough job where he worked, said, "Why not? That's part of my married and family life! You think I'd do that if it wasn't for my wife and kids?"

Good insight! He realized that what he did, his job, only made sense because it was motivated by the love he had for his wife and children. So, everything we do comes under spiritual stewardship as it flows from our interior life, from the love we bear for Christ and share with His Bride, the Church. St. Francis de Sales articulated this principle when he insisted that holiness must happen in the work we do and in the place we live.

X. The Final Component: Keeping Ever in View the Call to Holiness

Our goal is nothing less than a reordering of life through the sacraments, which will configure us in an irrevocable, radical way to Christ. That we may be good, holy, happy, healthy, learned, zealous, selfless, committed faithful is the goal of our spiritual growth.

I have two notes of caution, however. First, growth in holiness is not our accomplishment, but a pure gift from God. The Lord does it, not me! One of the great heresies rampant in our society is Pelagianism — believing that we can earn, deserve, or achieve our salvation. Such an approach leads to discouragement on the one hand, and self-righteousness or religious formalism on the other. These ten steps of spiritual stewardship I just went through are not cozy little acts we perform to produce holiness — they are simply tried-and-true ways we open up in humility to let the Lord in to do His work in, on, for, and, often, in spite of us!

Holiness is a mystery. It will always elude us. The moment we think we have it made, we'd better start from scratch; the moment we want to walk tall, we'd best get down on our knees, and the minute we think we're without sin, we've just committed the biggest one!

Second, to use the words of Sister Bridge McKenna, "The road inward to spiritual growth always results in a U-turn outward in love for others." In more classical terminology, the spiritual journey *ad intra* results in a life of love *ad extra*, to others. Our stewardship of the Spirit is never a soothing benefice we cling to, but an inspiration to love humankind better. As St. Paul says, "For in Christ Jesus neither circumcision nor uncircumcision is of any avail, but faith working through love" (Gal. 5:6). The Jesus who calls us to spiritual ecstasy on Mt. Tabor likewise invites us to the pouring out of self on Mt. Calvary.

The *Suscipe* of St. Ignatius of Loyola sums it up:

> Take, O Lord, and receive all my liberty, my memory, my understanding and my whole will. Thou hast given me all that I am and all that I possess. I surrender it all to Thee that Thou mayest dispose of it according to Thy will. Give me only Thy love and Thy grace; with these I will be rich enough, and will have no more to desire.

On the evening of that day, the first day of the week, the doors being shut where the disciples were, for fear of the Jews, Jesus came and stood among them and said to them, "Peace be with you." When he had said this, he showed them his hands and his side. Then the disciples were glad when they saw the Lord. Jesus said to them again, "Peace be with you. As the Father has sent me, even so I send you." And when he had said this, he breathed on them, and said to them, "Receive the Holy Spirit. If you forgive the sins of any, they are forgiven; if you retain the sins of any, they are retained." Now Thomas, one of the twelve, called the Twin, was not with them when Jesus came. So the other disciples told him, "We have seen the Lord." But he said to them, "Unless I see in his hands the print of the nails, and place my finger in the mark of the nails, and place my hand in his side, I will not believe." Eight days later, his disciples were again in the house, and Thomas was with them. The doors were shut, but Jesus came and stood among them, and said, "Peace be with you." Then he said to Thomas, "Put your finger here, and see my hands; and put out your hand, and place it in my side; do not be faithless, but believing." Thomas answered him, "My Lord and my God!" Jesus said to him, "Have you believed because you have seen me? Blessed are those who have not seen and yet believe."

— JN. 20:19–29

CHAPTER 2

✠

Faith

*D*uring my third parish assignment, my pastor happened to be one of the auxiliary bishops of the Archdiocese of St. Louis, George J. Gottwald. By that time, Bishop Gottwald was nearing retirement, rather worn out from nearly fifty years as a priest and twenty-five as a bishop. He loved to linger at the table and speak of the Second Vatican Council, but he was less than enthusiastic in speaking about the other critical period in his life, the nine months he served as apostolic administrator of the archdiocese following the death of Cardinal Joseph Ritter in June 1967.

The years immediately following the council were climactic times: a lot of good, creative, vibrant, promising movement in the Church, all prompted by the genuine call for reform by the council; but also, unfortunately, a lot of doubt, error, hurt, confusion, and downright silliness. At the height of all this, Bishop Gottwald, a very effective but very plain country pastor who became an auxiliary bishop out of sheer obedience, was thrust into leadership.

One of his many crises was the state of the seminary. One-fourth of the priest faculty left the priesthood, the student body was decimated by departures, and the theology being taught was anything but of the Church. The priests who remained on the faculty announced they wanted to join an ecumenical theologate, since, according to their interpretation of the council, it was useless to teach Catholic theology — since such a thing probably no longer existed.

They demanded the presence of the apostolic administrator at what was really a "campus demonstration" in the early spring of 1968, where they came to present him with their list of demands in front of the obligatory TV cameras.

Into this lion's den walked Bishop George Gottwald, shy, nervous, wishing he was still an unknown pastor in the Ozark hills of southern Missouri. The leader of the faculty and students informed the bishop that Kenrick Seminary might as well close, since the whole enterprise of priestly formation and Catholic theology was up for grabs. In response, the bishop offered the comment that, even with the legitimate questioning and probing of the council, there were still clear, consistent truths that had to be taught any future priest.

"Hah!" snickered the faculty spokesman. "I dare you to tell me what we can possibly teach our students now that has not changed, that will not change, that can be stated with any amount of conviction at all! I dare you to tell me!"

The bishop's mouth went dry, he recalls, as all eyes were on him, as the microphones clicked on and cameras whirled for a sound bite, as they waited for him to take the dare! And what did he answer?

"I believe in God, the Father Almighty, Creator of heaven and earth; and in Jesus Christ, His only Son, Our Lord: who was conceived by the Holy Ghost, born of the Virgin Mary; suffered under Pontius Pilate, was crucified, died, and was buried. He descended into hell; the third day He arose again from the dead; He ascended into heaven, sitteth at the right hand of God the Father Almighty; from thence He shall come to judge the living and the dead. I believe in the Holy Ghost, the Holy Catholic Church, the communion of saints, the forgiveness of sins, the resurrection of the body, and life everlasting. Amen."

The Apostles' Creed! A fundamental formula of faith expressed by the Church from near the beginning. This, my friends, was a man of *faith*: In the midst of doubt, ridicule, snickering, and confusion, he dared to state that there are certain truths that can always be counted upon because they come from God and not from us!

Faith. A steward carefully takes stock of what gifts, what treasures, what items he has at his disposal, realizing that he needs to draw upon them continually. We are stewards, and is there a more priceless gift in our interior storehouse than that of *faith*? Should we perhaps take stock?

"Faith," the Epistle to the Hebrews instructs us, "is the assurance of things hoped for, the conviction of things not seen." (Heb. 11:1) Yes, in spite of the aimlessness, contradiction, and skepticism around us, our faith allows us to cling to certain things with steadfastness: God exists! He loves us passionately! He has revealed truths to us! He has sent his Son as "the way, the truth, and the life" (Jn. 14:6)! His Son has saved us by His death and resurrection, and is still alive, powerful, with us! Our hearts are steadfast in this faith! Our faith assures us these propositions are true based not on cold, clinical evidence, but on simple, childlike, humble trust in a Father who will never mislead us.

Faith, of course, has as its object not propositions and doctrines directly, but a *person*, namely Jesus the Christ. We believe in Him, and thence flows our belief in what He and His Church have taught.

Many of you have children, and you love the *faith* they have in you as their parents. It's not rational but spontaneous and natural, part of their being. Children know that . . .

- when they cry, you will come;
- when they are scared, you will hold them;
- when they are hungry, you will feed them;
- when they are lonely, you will go to them.

Faith . . . and such is our faith in the Lord. Charles de Foucauld realized this when he wrote:

> The moment I realized that God existed, I could not do otherwise than to live for him alone. . . . Faith strips the mask from the world and reveals God in everything. It makes nothing impossible and renders meaningless such words as anxiety, fear, and danger, so that the believer goes through life calmly and peacefully, with profound joy — like a child hand in hand with his mother.

How tragic it would be if we took this admittedly primitive aspect of our lives — *faith* — for granted! Hardly careful stewardship! I propose one of the reasons we stumble and fall, or why we shrivel up into careless, crabby, comfortable, lazy people, has everything to do with *faith*!

When I was in college, a priest I'd admired immensely as a boy in my parish left the priesthood. I was very upset. He sent me a letter that I still read on occasion, in which he said, "Yes, I have lost my priestly vocation, but, I must admit, I lost my faith years ago. And there is no one more miserable than a priest who has no faith!" How right he was!

As Paul wrote Timothy: "But, as for you, man of God . . . aim at righteousness, godliness, faith . . ." (1 Tim. 6:11-12). "Follow the pattern of the sound words which you have heard from me, in the faith and love which are in Christ Jesus; guard the truth that has been entrusted to you by the Holy Spirit who dwells within us." (2 Tim. 1:13–14).

The story is told of nationalist leader Mahatma Gandhi of India: A young mother traveled eleven hours from a distant part of India to meet him and to ask his help with her troubled three-year-old boy, who was unruly, hyperactive, sleepless, always rambunctious.

"Tell me everything about him," Gandhi replied. "Tell me what he says, what he wears, what he eats, how he plays, what he dreams, with whom he plays outside." The mother did. Gandhi sat silent and said, "I know the difficulty, but I cannot tell you for a month. Come back then."

The mother made the arduous eleven-hour journey exactly a month later, and said to Gandhi, "What is wrong with my boy?" The holy man replied, "He eats too much sugar. Do not let him eat sugar and he'll be fine."

The woman, while relieved to find out the cure, was irritated and said, "If the answer was so simple, why did I have to make this terrible journey again? Why didn't you just tell me that a month ago?"

"Ah," Gandhi replied, "I could not tell you yet at that time, because I was still eating sugar."

I guess that's the eastern version of *nemo dat quod non habet* ("no one gives what he does not possess")! He knew he'd better first do what he was going to prescribe.

We spend a lot of time telling others, "Have faith!" Well, do *we* have it? Are we ourselves people of *faith*?

How scandalous it is when priests weaken the very faith that their people look to them to uphold, by how they live, what they say, what they do or do not do. These days people are faced with countless priests who ridicule their faith, who publicly criticize the magisterium and dismiss the truths of our Church.

I remember concelebrating midnight Mass one Christmas at the parish where my family now lives, only to hear the priest tell the people during his homily that the Gospel they just heard — one of the most moving in Scripture, one religious sociologists tell us evokes the most enduring of godly sentiments, the story of the first Christmas — was all fable. All made up. Probably never happened. Can you believe it?

I recall being at a Rite of Christian Initiation of Adults session where a gentleman asked the priest-presenter to explain a bit more the doctrine of the "real presence," whereupon he answered that this doctrine was not at all stable, but was being questioned and reformulated by the more enlightened theologians of the day.

As my mentor Monsignor John Tracy Ellis used to say, "No, the Church does not have all the answers, but she sure has more than any other institution on the face of the earth!" And, for God's sake, should not all her people be loyal to her and in love with her?

At the zenith of the Church's year, the Easter Vigil, Holy Mother Church asks everyone to consider the same question: Are we people of *faith?* Taking the Apostles' Creed part by part, she drives home the question *do you believe?* I submit that it is an essential part of spiritual stewardship for us to ask ourselves these questions ceaselessly as we examine our consciences about faith.

Do we believe in God? I hope so! But, do we believe in a God who is intimately involved in our lives, who has revealed himself and truths about himself and how He wants us to live? Who took flesh in the womb of the Blessed Virgin Mary, who really was born, lived, suffered, died, rose again, ascended into heaven, and sent His Spirit?

Do we believe in a God who has created us in His own image and likeness and who has destined us for eternity, an eternity with Him or without Him? Who breathed into us an immortal soul, which gives us identity and personhood, and can hold the very life of God imparted to us in the incomparable gift called sanctifying grace?

Do we believe God is alive and powerful in the prayers He answers and in the Church born from the opened side of His Son, that He continues to act in His seven sacraments — which really work and accomplish what they signify; that by baptism we became children of God and temples of the Holy Spirit; that in Eucharist we really and truly receive Our Lord, body, blood, soul, and divinity; that in the sacrament of penance our sins are really forgiven; that He continues to teach in the Scripture and Tradition of the Church, carefully guarded by the successors of the apostles, our bishops, especially the successor of St. Peter?

Do I believe that God has personally cherished me and called me from the moment of my conception, that He has a plan for me, that He has called me to follow His Son, who is my Lord and Savior? That He knows me better than I know myself, passionately loves me still, and is beckoning me to serve Him and His Church faithfully?

Do I believe that I have an irrevocable, total, permanent commitment to Christ and His Church that actually configures me to Jesus as head, shepherd, and spouse of His Church?

Acknowledge the pivotal importance of this question: Do I really believe? Especially in an age of doubt, cynicism, skepticism, which holds that only those things verifiable under a microscope or evident in a mathematical equation are true . . . in an age that holds that *faith* is at best a curious eccentricity for weak, unstable people, at worst a superstitious sham keeping people in bondage, do I really believe?

We are people of strong faith or we are nothing! For there is nothing more pitiable than a Christian without faith — and there are many. With faith we crave prayer, spiritual growth! With faith we eagerly respond to the promptings of grace and live virtuous, moral lives! With faith we are zealous and generous to others! With faith it all makes sense; we have peace and joy. As St. Augustine said, "There will be peace and tranquility in the Christian heart, but only as long as our faith is watchful. When our faith sleeps, we are in danger!"

Without faith — no meaning, no drive, no reason. We become cold, lazy, cynical crabs. The sacraments are empty — for we don't believe in them; sermons are boring — for we don't believe what we're hearing; and we futilely seek meaning in bottles, or sex, or golf clubs, or stocks, or shopping, or travel, or promotion, or ambition . . .

Without faith, we're setting ourselves up for a fall. For one day, sooner or later, the crisis will come. Maybe caused by fatigue over daily confrontations with evil and suffering; discouragement over our own weaknesses; maybe caused by failing in love, loneliness, sickness, or doubt. It will come, perhaps in the form of tortured questions: Is there a God? Is the Church from God? Am I a fool? Unless that faith is there, we've had it!

I love the way Thomas Merton, perhaps finding himself at one such moment of trial, yet relying on his faith, expressed it:

> My Lord God, I have no idea where I am going. I do not see the road ahead of me. I cannot know where it will end. Nor do I really know myself, and the fact that I think that I am following your will does not mean that I am actually doing so. But I believe that the desire to please you does in fact please you. And I hope I have that desire in all I am doing. I hope that I will never do anything apart from that desire. And I know that if I do this you will lead me by the right road though I may know nothing about it.

Therefore, I will trust you always though I may seem to be lost in the shadow of death. I will not fear, for you are ever with me, and you will never leave me to face my perils alone.

How then can we increase and protect our faith?

1. A pursuit of religious studies will enhance our faith. *Fides quaerens intellectum* ("Faith seeking understanding"), as St. Anselm defined it. We dread a stale, insipid, child*ish* defensive faith; we crave a strong, lively, confident, child*like* faith. Thus, we are not afraid to probe, wonder, question, think critically. As Pope Leo XIII said, "The Church is not afraid of the truth."

From this study, this critical, reflective probing, this wondering and listening, comes a faith with which we are so at home that we can express it simply, poetically, confidently, personally.

My first pastor said to me as I went over to school the first day to teach, "Now we'll see if you really learned your theology when you go in to teach first grade." How right he was!

2. Our prayer increases our faith, for, at its core, faith is a gift that is ours for the asking. Those magnificent prayers of the Gospel — "Lord, I do believe! Help my lack of faith!" "Lord, increase my faith!" — have been indispensable.

I recall giving instructions once to a professor of mathematics at Washington University in St. Louis. He was marrying a Catholic girl and sincerely wanted to join the Church. Never have I seen anyone try harder for faith! He never missed an instruction, devoured every catechism I gave him, asked tough questions, even read St. Thomas Aquinas' *Summa Theologica!* Still, no faith.

"Father, what can I do?" he asked in mental agony. It then dawned on me that we were both approaching faith as if it were a discipline, a course, knowledge to be digested. But it isn't, of course — it is a gift from God. So I said, "Have you prayed for faith, asking God to give it to you?"

"Well, no," he responded.

So he did, and I did. He was baptized . . . and his first son told me he wanted to be a priest. Pray for faith!

A past spiritual director once encouraged me to what he called a "prayer of articulation," where I would simply begin to tell the Lord what I believed, what I held dear, what I couldn't live without, what helped me get through — my faith. It has helped me.

3. Be careful about signs. We love to seek signs, exotic validations of our faith. Now, our Catholic tradition has always held that these things — apparitions, miracles, prophecies, stigmata — can *enhance* our faith but never take its place. And if all those externals caved in, really, so what? Our faith does not depend on them, but on *Him*. They're only the sauce, not the pasta.

4. Crisis, suffering — these can purify and strengthen our faith. I don't know if my faith was ever stronger than when I said the prayers after death over the still-warm body of my dad after he had dropped dead at work at fifty-one, with my mother sobbing beside me.

Faith is fine when we're healthy, but elusive when sick. Faith is not needed when we're fulfilled, content, satisfied — but do we ever need it when frustrated, worried, anxious, preoccupied! Comfort, ease, security can sometimes strangle it. As we hear in the Epistle of St. James: "Count it all joy, my brethren, when you meet various trials, for you know that the testing of your faith produces steadfastness" (Jas. 1:2–3).

5. We need the company, support, and encouragement of people who will sustain our faith. When I was rector at the North American College, we prayed with and for one another, worked for the same goals, discussed matters of faith, and hope-

fully provided one another with good examples. There we had advisers and spiritual directors who challenged us and probed us. I remember one of the first-year men telling me after about three weeks, "Father, it is so good to be with people who share my beliefs, where I'm not scared or embarrassed to talk about Jesus, or Mary, or prayer, or temptation, or worries." Thank God we have solidarity in prayer groups, consecration to Mary, unity in apostolates, and study.

What is more essential than faith?

I remember a meeting at the Venerable English College in Rome. There in the chapel is the famous portrait of the seminarians in the sixteenth century being sent to England as priests for what was almost certain martyrdom. Hundreds went from Rome back to England, where the Church was persecuted. Many were arrested on the dock disembarking the ship. They were warned, threatened, sent back to Europe . . . only to catch the next ship over. Dozens — hundreds — were harassed, imprisoned, tortured, brutally martyred . . . and the stories only encouraged their brothers preparing for the same fate. They kept going over. As one of them wrote: "Faith is readiness to die for Christ's sake, for his commandments, in the conviction that such death brings life; it is to regard poverty as riches, insignificance and nothingness as true fame and glory, and, having nothing, to be sure you possess all things. But, above all, faith is attainment of the invisible treasure of the knowledge of Christ."

On All Souls' Day at *Campo Verano*, Rome's main Catholic cemetery, I saw the memorial plaque for Joe Toomey, a man just a year behind me in the seminary from the Archdiocese of New York. Recalling him led me to check his files, because I remember to this day a letter he had sent us. I was pleased to find it:

Dear Charlie and my friends at NAC,

These past two weeks have been most trying. While I was in the hospital the doctors kept telling me that they were pushing for complete success. All of those terrible side effects returned and I fought them with renewed courage and hope. I firmly believed that the chemicals would destroy the remaining cancer.

Five days after my release from the hospital, I took a chest X-ray and was shocked by the results. The news was heartbreaking; I had made only very slight progress. The doctor very sadly told me that soon I would have to resume the nauseating weekly therapy for an indeterminable amount of time.

This news caused me to fall into a deep state of depression for a number of days. But God would not allow me to wallow in senseless despair. He kept reminding me that I must seek strength through the sacraments. Your prayers and those of my friends at home also gave me that much needed psychological and spiritual power to face a possibly long future of constant physical discomfort.

I cried tonight thinking of you all, of how much I long to return to the college. Perhaps the Lord permits me to suffer temporarily in order to add a stronger dimension of spirituality to your lives and the lives of all whom I meet. This is a joyful purpose, an actuation of true love.

Please continue to write me; I hope to see you next fall.

Cardinal Cooke ordained Joe a deacon on his deathbed, and he died seven weeks after that moving letter.

What can explain that letter but faith? What can possibly explain what we hope to spend our lives doing as Christians but faith?

Let us pray the Act of Faith:

> O my God, I firmly believe that thou art one God in three divine Persons, Father, Son, and Holy Spirit. I believe that thy divine Son became man, and died for our sins and that he will come to judge the living and the dead. I believe these and all the truths which the Holy Catholic Church teaches because thou hast revealed them, who can neither deceive nor be deceived.

On that day, when evening had come, he said to them, "Let us go across to the other side." And leaving the crowd, they took him with them in the boat, just as he was. And other boats were with him. And a great storm of wind arose, and the waves beat into the boat, so that the boat was already filling. But he was in the stern, asleep on the cushion; and they woke him and said to him, "Teacher, do you not care if we perish?" And he awoke and rebuked the wind, and said to the sea, "Peace! Be still!" And the wind ceased, and there was a great calm. He said to them, "Why are you afraid? Have you no faith?" And they were filled with awe, and said to one another, "Who then is this, that even wind and sea obey him?"

— MK. 4:35–41

CHAPTER 3

———✦———

Hope

At Kenrick-Glennon Seminary in St. Louis, there was a senior in the college program named Michael Esswein. If *60 Minutes* had come to us wanting to do a report on "the model seminarian," we would have unanimously put forth Michael: he was holy, intelligent, handsome, outgoing, considerate, respected by his peers, a good soccer player — "man of the year" candidate!

Michael came from a very big, happy family. His older sister was a nun, and, during spring break, the first Friday of March 1993, Michael, one of his brothers, and his mom and dad got into the family van to drive from St. Louis to Connecticut to visit that sister. Outside of Youngstown, Ohio, they ran into bad weather and hit an icy spot on the interstate; the van skidded off the roadway, tumbled down an embankment, and landed upside-down.

Michael was trapped, unconscious, upside-down, in the back seat for fifty minutes while the emergency team worked to free him. It was clear he was hurt severely, and he was taken to the nearest hospital for surgery. For eight hours the surgeons assessed and tried to repair the damage, and then came out to inform the family — who had not been injured, by the way — that, while Michael had indeed survived, his spine was irreparably damaged, and he would be paralyzed from the neck down for the rest of his life.

When he woke up, his first question was, "How is the rest of the family?" Then, seeing the apprehension on the faces of everyone around him, and sensing his powerless body telling him that something was drastically wrong, he asked, "Will I still be able to be a priest?" That's the kind of young man Michael Esswein was.

Anyway, the Sunday evening following the accident, Michael's home parish planned a prayer service for his healing. St. Stephen's Parish was standing-room-only, and the pastor led us in a moving hour of prayer for Michael, specifically entrusting Michael to the Sacred Heart of Jesus. This made perfect sense since the Esswein family had devotion to Our Lord under that title . . . since Michael's sister (whom they were going to visit) was a student at Cor Jesu Academy, a Catholic girl's college preparatory school . . . and since the accident occurred on a First Friday. Never have I participated in a more intense hour of intercessory prayer. At the end, with a voice full of optimism, the pastor announced, "When Michael returns, we will reassemble for a prayer service of thanksgiving."

After ten weeks in that Ohio hospital, following two subsequent surgeries and intense therapy, Michael indeed did return, and, sure enough, the same throng gathered at St. Stephen's for prayers of thanksgiving. But a pall of gloom and pessimism descended as Michael was wheeled down the main aisle; he was able to move only his head, and that only barely, to greet the congregation. Once he was up the newly installed ramp to the sanctuary, the service began. When the time came for the Scripture reading, Michael himself proclaimed the Gospel cited at the beginning of this chapter. At its conclusion, as we all sat to listen intently, Michael spoke.

"You all came here for a service of thanksgiving," he said, "but as I was wheeled up the aisle, you all thought, 'Thanksgiving for what? This young man is a quadriplegic, and will be for the rest of his life. His promising future is destroyed. This is hardly an answer to our prayers!' "

You could have heard a pin drop in that jammed church. Then Michael continued.

"I must admit to you that I have felt the same way every once in a while these last ten weeks since the accident. In other words, like the apostles in the Gospel in the midst of that overwhelming storm, we are tempted to think Our Lord is asleep and couldn't care less. *Hope,* my friends," he bellowed out, "*hope* is the gift that keeps us going when we think Jesus is asleep, and let us thank God for that great gift of hope!"

That was the most moving sermon on hope I have ever heard. I was sitting next to the chancellor of the archdiocese who whispered to me, "Let's ordain that man tomorrow."

"Hope is the virtue that keeps us going when we are tempted to think that Jesus is asleep. . . ."

"For God alone my soul waits in silence, for my hope is from him. He only is my rock and my salvation, my fortress; I shall not be shaken" (Ps. 62:5–6).

I ask you to meditate with me precisely on hope. Earlier, I spoke about faith. Faith, of course, is the virtue by which we believe there is a God; hope is the virtue by which we trust that this God keeps his promises! "I am a man of hope," writes Belgian Cardinal Joseph Suenens, "not for human reasons nor from just natural optimism, but because I believe that the Lord is at work in my life, in the Church, and in the world, even when his name remains unheard."

Hope moves us to trust that the God in whom we believe will always love us and care for us, that He keeps his promises — not assuring us bliss, comfort, ease, perfection, fulfillment — but love, care, mercy, life.

I speak to you of *hope* for many reasons: Yes, every human being, certainly every Christian, needs *hope*. There are times when everything seems dark, cold, and damp, and spring is not evident—in such times we need a good chalk-talk on hope.

But, more importantly, *hope* — a deep, abiding, unflappable, calm yet noticeable *hope* — is essential for everyone!

"What oxygen is to the lungs," writes Swiss Protestant theologian Emil Brunner, "such is hope for the meaning of life."

Now, let's get basic. How do we get hope? Well, we cannot obtain it on our own. We can't *get* it . . . we are *given* it! *Hope* is a virtue given us by God at baptism, intensified by the other sacraments, fostered and protected through a strong interior life flowing from a vibrant faith, and strengthened in daily perseverance through the tribulations and adversity life unfailingly brings. True, *supernatural hope* can be bolstered through *natural* habits such as a good sense of humor, an upbeat personality, a cheerful, optimistic outlook on life, and a realistic admission in the midst of trial that "this, too, shall pass."

What is of the essence, though, is the cultivation of a strong spiritual life. You have probably heard the analogy of the hurricane — in the midst of the turbulence, destruction, and overwhelming force of the storm, there is the "eye of the hurricane," an island of peace, calm, serenity. Thus is our interior life: in the midst of the storm, winds of unpredictability, setback, crisis, tragedy, or just the plain daily grind that can overwhelm us, we harbor an inner space of peace, calm, and serenity, where the Lord dwells, from which *hope* comes. Our regimen of prayer, Eucharist, devotion, spiritual direction, spiritual reading, and the sacraments — this regimen is all directed to fostering this interior "eye of the hurricane" from which comes the *hope* to get us through what life brings.

You may have seen it, for instance, in Pope John Paul II. Those of you who have been privileged to attend his daily private Mass know how moving it is to see him locked in intense prayer prior to, during, and after Mass. Those who seek the reason for his immense strength, determination, and *hope* need look no further than this.

I detected it in Tom Mucha, a young man who underwent chemotherapy for leukemia, when I talked to him on the phone several years ago. In the midst of severe pain, with chances of life fifty-fifty at best, he demonstrated an inner calm, a sense of *hope*, that must flow from a strong interior life which has been made durable by the crucible of suffering.

You see it exemplified in the life of a saint like Maximilian Kolbe, who, while stuffed in a cell with nine others slowly to die of starvation and thirst, exhibited a calm, a peace, a *hope* that inspired his co-condemned while infuriating, yet baffling, the guards.

This dependable interior life, providing the "eye of the hurricane," flows from the faith we spoke of before, a childlike trust that all is in God's providential hands, that nothing is impossible for him; that with him all things are possible; that, although his will can be disregarded by some, his kingdom can be stopped by no one; that ultimately all will make sense because, as St. Paul writes, ". . . in everything God works for good with those who love him, who are called according to his purpose" (Rom. 8:28).

The Fundamentalists can teach us something about this. Flip through the offbeat channels on TV or radio at home on Sunday and odds are you'll hear some reverend yelling, "The victory has been won! The war is over! There are still some skirmishes we must fight, but these are only the last gasps of a defeated enemy! Alleluia!"

All they're saying is what St. Bernard said: "If Christ is with us, who is against us? You can fight with confidence where you are sure of victory. With Christ and for Christ victory is certain."

"For God alone my soul waits in silence, for my hope is from him. He only is my rock and my salvation, my fortress; I shall not be shaken" (Ps. 62:5–6).

I love the story of Pope John XXIII told by Monsignor Loris Capovilla, his private secretary. Every night about midnight, before going to bed, Pope John would kneel before the Blessed Sacrament. There he would rehearse the problems he had encountered that day: the bishop who came in to tell of his priests massacred and his nuns raped in the Congo; the world leader who came to tell him of his country's plight in war and asking his help; the sick who came to be blessed; the refugees writing for help; the newest round of oppression behind the Iron Curtain. As Pope John would go over each problem, examining his conscience to see if he had responded to each with effective decisions and appropriate help, he would finally take a deep breath and say, "Well, I did the best I could. . . . It's your Church, Lord! I'm going to bed. Good night."

Now that's a man of *hope*! "When tempted to lose *hope*," says the Curé of Ars St. John Vianney, "I have only one resource: to throw myself at the foot of the tabernacle like a little dog at the foot of his master."

"Trust in him at all times, O people; pour out your heart before him; God is a refuge for us" (Ps. 62:8).

Sometimes we need to stay steadfast in hope for a long time, too. My first Lent as a parish priest, the president of the Men's Club said, "Father, you're supposed to give us an evening of recollection in Lent." I should have known by his lack of enthusiasm that there was hardly going to be trouble finding a parking space. Nevertheless, I worked for hours over three talks on characters from the Stations of the Cross. The big night came — two men showed up. Needless to say, I hardly needed the microphone. Two men! I was crushed. I didn't get much help from the pastor when I went back to the rectory and he told me, "Oh, I should have told you those never work."

Then, twelve years later, I visited a woman from that parish in bed helpless with Lou Gehrig's disease. Her husband was so tender with her, caring for her, not leaving her side. As he showed me to the door, I told him how I admired his devotion to his wife. He said, "Oh, Father, I'm just trying to be that Simon of Cyrene you talked about." I looked at him, confused. "Yeah, remember that Lenten evening of recollection when you told us that just as Simon of Cyrene helped Our Lord carry his cross, we do the same every time we help somebody else carry theirs? I'm just trying to help Ramona carry hers."

This kind of thing is worth the wait . . . and hope helps us wait.

"For God alone my soul waits in silence, for my hope is from him. He only is my rock and my salvation, my fortress; I shall not be shaken" (Ps. 62:5–6).

We are tempted to put our hope in a lot of things, and these begin to consume us. Some are good things: we place trust in friends, in our reputation, in the just satisfaction that comes from a job well done. But you know the day will come when even those legitimate, good objects of trust will let us down; so if we put total trust in even these legitimate things, we will one day be disappointed.

Is there anyone sadder than someone who put all his trust in the hope of career advancement and ends his years bitter and resentful?

If you read the life of Archbishop John Ireland of New York, one of the towering characters of American Catholic history, you see how he ended his brilliant career terribly disappointed because the "red hat" never came.

Even our friends will eventually move, or drift away, or let us down ... we cherish them and need them, but we cannot place all our *hope* in them either.

In our life, we cannot *hope* in big salaries, signs of favor from our employers, wide acclaim. If they come, we accept them with Ignatian indifference, grateful, but able to get along just as well without them, for "we place not our trust in princes."

As rector at the North American College, I would tell first-year men on the first day they arrived, "You have left home, family, friends, security, predictability.... Everything has changed but one thing — your faith in and relationship with Jesus Christ: He is the same yesterday, today, and tomorrow! And perhaps the genius of study here in Rome, away from all that is familiar and reliable, is to teach us that He and He alone is the ultimate source of our *hope* — to count on anything or anyone else in this life will ultimately lead to disappointment."

"...if riches increase, set not your heart upon them. ... power belongs to God" (Ps. 62:10–11).

A most crucial virtue flows from *hope*, and that is *perseverance*. Be faithful, always be faithful! To keep at it, not to flag, to continue the good fight, to remain faithful, to *persevere*, even in the midst of doubt, confusion, frustration — that flows from *hope*.

We *hope* that the good work begun in us by God is brought to perfection, that such a prayer is being answered every day of our lives. The ancient principle is that God never asks us to do something without giving us the graces necessary to accomplish it. That gives *hope*; that motivates us to *persevere* in our Christian lives.

Hope is particularly needed in our prayer. The patience, persistence, and perseverance that the Master tells us must accompany fruitful prayer all spring from the virtue of *hope*. The worst mistake we can make when we are having a difficulty in prayer is to give up, to lose *hope*. There is no use denying that prayer is at times boring, unproductive, stale, full of distractions, and just plain tough. Here is where *hope* is needed:

- to trust that God is listening even when there is no response;
- to *hope* he is there when it seems he has abandoned us;
- to trust that our efforts at prayer are producing some invisible fruit when all visible signs of success are not there;
- to *hope* that "wasting time with the Lord" — as Thomas Merton defined prayer — is actually more productive than getting some practical work accomplished.

Remember St. John of the Cross. His practice was to record what happened in his prayer each day in his journal. For a long period in his life, probably his "dark night of the soul," he recorded one word: *nada. Nothing!* What went on in my prayer today? *Nada!* Not one day, but days, weeks, months, *nada!* But *hope* he kept, trusting that something would break. And with hope he prevailed, as he is looked to now as one of those rare creatures who actually reached the heights of mystical prayer.

Along the same line, *hope* helps us in our struggle with sin. Whatever evil inclination we battle — impatience, gossip, laziness, impurity, a bad temper, a judgmental tongue, whatever — we make some progress and then fall, and at times are tempted to despair and give up our journey to perfection. Never! A wise confessor once told me, "In the end, what counts is not how many times we have succeeded or failed, but how we have begun again after a failure." That takes *hope*! Archbishop Fulton Sheen reminds us that there are no plains in our spiritual life, only hills and valleys, and the key to growth in holiness is not to lose hope when in the valley.

In the First Letter of Peter we read, "Always be prepared to make a defense to any one who calls you to account for the *hope* that is in you" (1 Pet. 3:15; emphasis added).

You see, a vibrant *hope* is contagious and will attract people. Its fruits are calmness, cheerfulness, tranquility, a good sense of humor, freedom from anxiety — and these traits people find very attractive. So, people can be attracted to Jesus and his Church through her *hopeful* members. This is not some Pollyannaish, cheerleading, shallow optimism. This is a realistic, sturdy trust in God based on deep faith, born in experience, and bolstered by reason.

Such is the purpose for the Church's expectation that we are firmly grounded in the study of our Faith, precisely so we can, as St. Peter says, "be able to explain the reason for this *hope* of yours."

Not that we're "know-it-alls." People don't expect an answer, just a reassurance that there is indeed an answer, a reason, which someday, somewhere, will be clear, even if hidden now. That gives them *hope*.

I remember once at the funeral of a one-year-old baby who had died suddenly of what appeared to be a simple cold, the child of two very active parishioners who had tried for six years to have this baby. The church was overflowing, the parents beyond consolation. The pastor took a long time after the Gospel before beginning his homily and finally said, "If you all think I'm going to explain to you why little Matthew died, you're going to be disappointed. I don't really know why Matthew died. Even with *hope* in a loving God it makes little sense. But without that *hope* it makes absolutely no sense at all."

The parents told me those were the only words that made any sense at all in that dark time.

"The most beautiful Credo is the one we pronounce in our hour of darkness," said St. Padre Pio.

Our Ultimate Hope

We must never be afraid to speak of heaven, where our hopes will ultimately be fulfilled.

When I lived in Washington, D.C., I used to help at the Gift of Peace House run by the Missionaries of Charity for dying AIDS victims. Sometimes I would baptize, anoint, pray with, or hear the confessions of men close to death. The sisters would always be so excited to report to me when a man had died after professing faith, contrition, asking God's mercy, for then they were confident, they told me, that he went to heaven. "That is why we do this work," one of the sisters explained, "to get souls to heaven."

Yes, they cleaned those helpless, dying men, bandaged their wounds, changed their diapers, hand-fed them, and cared for people no one else wanted. But their motive was to help a soul reach heaven.

We have grown embarrassed about discussing heaven, perhaps afraid we will come across as overly pious, too otherworldly, or unconcerned about the problems of this life. But sometimes the burdens of this life can so crush people that they long to discuss that place "where every tear will be wiped away," and, if we won't or can't do it, who will?

As we pray in the antiphon for the *Benedictus* on the feast of St. Agnes: "What I longed for, I now see: what I hoped for, I now possess; in heaven I am espoused to Him whom on earth I loved with all my heart."

"We did not dare to breathe a prayer or to give our anguish scope! Something was dead in each of us, and what was dead was *Hope*," writes the Irish writer Oscar Wilde, and this seems to characterize us today.

I remember seeing Cardinal Bernard Law being interviewed on TV outside the White House, where he had just met with President George H. Bush on averting what seemed to be sure war with Iraq. "Have you lost hope, Cardinal?" one of the reporters shouted.

"I'm in the business of hope!" responded the cardinal.

Yes, we are all "in the business of hope." We are those who, in the boat at times about to capsize in the midst of the storm, keep on going even when it seems that Jesus is asleep.

Let us pray:

O my God, relying on your infinite promises, I hope to obtain the pardon of my sins, the help of your grace, and life everlasting, through the merits of Jesus Christ, my Lord and my redeemer. Amen.

Have this mind among yourselves, which is yours in Christ Jesus, who, though he was in the form of God, did not count equality with God a thing to be grasped, but emptied himself, taking the form of a servant, being born in the likeness of men. And being found in human form he humbled himself and became obedient unto death, even death on a cross. Therefore God has highly exalted him and bestowed on him the name which is above every name, that at the name of Jesus every knee should bow, in heaven and on earth and under the earth, and every tongue confess that Jesus Christ is Lord, to the glory of God the Father.

— Phil. 2:5–11

—✠—

CHAPTER 4

Humility

The now deceased Passionist Scripture scholar Barnabas Ahern gave one of the most poignant retreat conferences I ever attended. He began by raising the question, "What was Our Lord's favorite virtue?"

Faith?... certainly high up there...

Hope?... rank it near the top...

Charity?... think how often the Master spoke of love...

Justice?... a case could be made...

But all of these pale, and take second place to what Father Ahern posited to be Our Lord's favorite virtue — humility.

Humility is the pivotal virtue of the interior life, the favorite of Jesus, held up by all the saints and ascetical theologians as the *sine qua non* of all progress on the road to perfection. In the simple words of St. Thérèse of Lisieux, "The beginning of all holiness is humbly admitting that without God we can do nothing, but that, with, in, and through him, everything is possible!"

The Gospels are, of course, odes to humility, as we see on every page the divine preference for the humble:

- the sick over the healthy,
- those who lack over those who have,
- the lowly virgin rather than the exquisite socialite,
- the oafish fishermen rather than the sophisticated scribes,
- the poor over the rich,

- the nerds to the in-crowd,
- the sinner to the snug,
- children to adults . . .

"Lord, that I may see!" chants the blind beggar . . .

"If I can but touch the tassel on his cloak!" whispers the sick woman in the crowd . . .

"Lord, I am not worthy," admits the centurion . . .

"Just the scraps from the table," begs the Canaanite woman . . .

"Lord, remember me when you come into your kingdom," utters Dismas . . .

All humble prayers that move His Sacred Heart, the heart He himself describes as gentle and humble.

Why is humility so prized by Jesus?

Maybe because His mission as our redeemer was precisely to save us from the opposite of humility — pride — the original sin by which our first parents felt they could get along just fine without God. As St. Augustine observes, "It was pride that caused the Fall. . . . If you ask me what are the ways to God, I would tell you the first is humility, the second is humility, the third is humility. . . ."

Maybe because His Incarnation was the most sublime act of humility ever, as God the Son, the Eternal Word, the second Person of the Blessed Trinity, took flesh and became man. "Humility," writes St. Bernard, "is the mother of salvation."

Maybe humility is so valued by Christ because of its very definition. St. Thomas Aquinas says in the *Summa Theologica* that humility means seeing ourselves as God sees us: knowing that every good we have comes from him as pure gift, that we depend on him for everything. Is this not the "poverty of spirit" listed as first in the eight beatitudes? And, since Jesus literally saw with the eyes of God, He especially cherished those who did the same. St. Vincent de Paul expressed it well: "The reason why God is so great a lover of humility is that he is a great lover of truth. Humility is nothing but truth while pride is nothing but lying.... The very moment God sees us fully convinced of our nothingness, he reaches out his hand to us."

One of the welcome developments in contemporary spirituality is an appreciation of the twelve-step program of Alcoholics Anonymous. No one can recover from alcoholism, claims that extraordinarily successful program, until one admits with disarming honesty and humility that one is absolutely helpless over drink and entrusts one's recovery to a Higher Power. Apply that to all sin, darkness, addiction, struggle, vice, evil, and weakness, and begin to live, begin to grow... but to do that takes humility.

In our Christian understanding there is this humility before God, and then there is a humility before others — to put others first, to battle egotism, to shun honor, acclaim, and attention, to rejoice when others are preferred over us. This humility before God and others is one of the toughest virtues to cultivate, but crucially necessary.

Let me enumerate what I feel are particular dangers, and then practical helps, to this cultivation of humility.

First, some of the pitfalls on the road to humility.

The Pelagianism rampant in Catholic life — that is, to think we can achieve, or merit our own redemption, to think that salvation depends on us. Of course, we know that holiness, heaven, cannot be earned, but only given, to one who *humbly* admits that he needs God desperately and can never win divine favor on his own merits. Pelagianism stems, of course, from pride, the opposite of humility, an exaltation of human ability.

It's true that we are called to *do* so many things — attend Mass, pray, confess our sins, do acts of penance, strive for virtue

— and rightly are these duties a necessary part of our spiritual regimen. We do them, though, not to earn or produce holiness — that's Pelagianism — but to open ourselves *humbly* to the power of God's love.

A subtle form of Pelagianism is found today among some in the Church: the belief that the vigor, the orthodoxy, the salvation of the Church all depend on me. When I was a rector, I attended a rectors' meeting in England in 1995, where a number of my colleagues recalled a very beneficial encounter they had the year before with the prefect of the Congregation for Catholic Education, Cardinal Pio Laghi. One of the rectors commented that he worried that some seminarians and younger priests felt they personally had a divine mandate to save the Church from rampant heresy and modernism.

Cardinal Laghi replied, "Yes, I always worry about a young man who feels he is the Church's savior. The Church happens already to have one!"

That's not limited to young priests. We had an old pastor in St. Louis who really believed the parish, the diocese, if not the entire Church, would crumble if he did not keep it going with his constant work. Because of this, he rarely took a vacation, and when he did, he would return early, frantically asking his assistants, "Is everything all right? Did anything happen?" — almost upset that the parish, diocese, and Church universal survived rather well during his absence. One year the senior assistant put up "For Sale" signs in front of the Church, rectory, and school when the pastor left to really drive the old man crazy when he got back!

You should know there will be some things in any parish that you will not be happy with, some practices or ways of doing things that are not perhaps the way you would do it — humbly accept them. I'm not talking about questions of faith and morals, but style, praxis, procedures. Humbly, gradually, patiently, gently insert yourself into parish life.

Humility! The Church already has a savior and, Pelagianism notwithstanding, I am not he!

A second pitfall in our pilgrimage to humility is pragmatism. Especially do we Americans pride ourselves on practicality, getting things done; we are task-oriented and feel everything is possible by sweat, work, and effort. An exaggerated sense of pragmatism can stifle humility. Yes, God wants our work and effort, but, "Unless the LORD builds the house, those who build it labor in vain" (Psalm 127:1).

We are not defined by what we do, how much we earn or produce, or what we achieve, but by who we are, and we are usually closest to God when we are weakest, emptiest, and lowest. To admit that takes humility . . . and can drive a pragmatist nuts.

The Lord and the Church say: Take your time! Wait! Prepare! Get ready! Yes, we prefer the microwave — put the food in, push the button; in a matter of minutes, the meal is ready. The Lord and the Church prefer the crock-pot: let it brew, stew, be seasoned, mellowed, for hours, then have your meal. And the food from the crock-pot beats the stuff from a microwave any day.

Is there a better example than the Master himself? Thirty years of unrecorded preparation for three years of active ministry. No pragmatist planned that timetable! February is traditionally dedicated to the "Hidden Life of Jesus" . . . those thirty years of quiet, prayer, preparation, anticipation, listening, growing, subject to his Blessed Mother and St. Joseph — what humility! I recommend meditation on the "Hidden Life of Jesus" to those who are tempted to get frustrated with the slow, crock-pot pace of life.

This patient humility — countering a more aggressive pragmatism — is evident in the lives of those who are happy and peaceful where they are. "The fear of the Lord in training for wisdom and humility goes before honors. In his mind a man plans his course, but the Lord directs his steps," teaches Proverbs.

A third trap on the road to humility: an inordinate stress on personal rights. We Americans are grateful that we are citizens of a country derived from an insistence on the rights of individuals — and rightly so; we belong to a Church that champions human rights, shepherded by a pastor known as the world's most forceful defender of human rights — thank God! I am not talking of this, but about the complex that leads us to believe that we've got things coming to us, that we deserve special treatment and preference. Thus, we get down when not given the recognition we feel should be coming to us. My boss doesn't appreciate me, my spouse doesn't realize all the work I do, the children don't realize how lucky they are to have me!

We had a great priest in St. Louis who was well-known for his zeal and gentle humility. He was a pastor of a poor, struggling parish. One of the plums in the archdiocese opened up and most of the priests stayed near their phones waiting for Cardinal Carberry to call and ask them to take the plush parish.

This humble priest got the call. "I want you to be pastor of St. Clement's," the cardinal said.

"Eminence, thanks, but I'm happy here, and there are dozens more who would be much more effective."

"Now I know I want you," responded the cardinal. "I have before me twenty-three letters from men asking for the place; you don't think you're worthy — you're now the pastor."

Some of the saddest of priests are those who feel they have been overlooked. They have set their hearts on advancement in the Church and ecclesiastical honors. "Scarlet Fever" it is sometimes called, and it is a dangerous virus in the clerical life.

This exaggerated insistence on "my rights, my prerogatives," ultimately leads to a dangerous spiritual and emotional malady, that of feeling sorry for myself. This self-centered licking of wounds, rehearsing the ways we have been overlooked, taken for granted, unappreciated — look out! That's when we're setting ourselves up for a fall — in the areas of sexuality; drinking; damaging association with others who will join us in the negative, cynical carping that afflicts those who feel their rights have been violated.

Humility teaches us to put all this in perspective, as we admit that we really deserve nothing at all, and that, in the long run, honors, attention, and prestige are dangerous and better off avoided. In the words of St. Paul, "If I am to boast, I boast in the cross of Our Lord Jesus Christ."

This exaggerated emphasis on personal rights is an overemphasis on *me*, which is the opposite of the way it should be. Mother Teresa, in her characteristic simplicity, says the proper order of priorities in life is J-O-Y:

J — Jesus
O — Others
Y — You

Humility makes us aware of our weakness, our frailty, our faults, that we recognize we need all the help we can get — from God, from others. So we are not afraid to get down on our knees and pray, to confide in friends, to open up to a spiritual director, to seek support from others, even to seek assistance from professionals in medicine or counseling.

A final (Lord knows there are more) pitfall I will mention: a proud rationalism that leads us to think we have to comprehend everything, that God owes us an explanation, and that our peanut brains are capable of understanding all there is, thus eliminating the awe and mystery of life.

Compare this to the humble prayer of Psalm 131:

O Lord, my heart is not lifted up,
my eyes are not raised too high.
I do not occupy myself with things
too great and too marvelous for me.
But I have calmed and quieted my soul,
like a child quieted at its mother's breast,
like a child that is quieted is my soul.

So the greatest theologian ever, St. Thomas Aquinas, surveying his life's work, said, "It's all straw when compared to the overwhelming mystery and majesty and mercy of God."

Enough of the dangers — how about some helps to humility?

No surprise that the first is prayer. As Bishop Fulton Sheen said, "Only the humble can pray, for prayer presumes we need someone and something." There's an old saying that the two most important lessons in life are, first, there is a God; second, I am not he! As the Lord spoke to St. Catherine of Siena, "You are she who is not, and I am who is!" Prayer acknowledges that.

I have found it helpful in my prayer to contemplate the eyes of Christ staring at me, piercing right through me: as he "looked hard" at the rich young man, as he gazed at the woman at the well, as he glared at Peter after the triple denial — the eyes of Christ piercing through us. No thought, word, or deed is hidden; he knows us better than we know ourselves. We are empty, open, poor, weak, broken before that gaze — and yet those eyes are loving, welcoming, accepting. That contemplation helps our humility.

In my first parish assignment, one of my Communion calls was a very prominent St. Louis woman who, the pastor told me, was terminally ill with cancer. When I called to set the time, she was very precise in saying I should not come before 11:30 a.m. on Friday. I found her looking remarkably well for a woman supposedly dying. Every Friday morning the same.

Well, one day, I was near her house, and decided to stop in unannounced. Her nurse opened the door, and, as I entered, I saw my Communion call gasp as she quickly tried to wheel herself out of my sight. . . . She was without any makeup, without any hair, yellowish in color, drawn and old, obviously dying. . . . It dawned on me that every Friday morning she had spent hours preparing herself to look presentable, and now I had surprised her and found her as she really was — weak, ugly, bald, yellow, old, and dying. She started to cry, "Oh, Father, I never wanted anyone to see me like this. I am so ashamed!"

All I could do was embrace her and assure her that I couldn't care less what she looked like, that I loved her and cared for her soul. With that we had a moving conversation about death, about suffering, about God.

That should be our posture of humility in prayer — the Lord sees us without sham, warts and all, dying, weak, sick, helpless, and afraid. No use impressing him. His eyes stare right through us.

Juliana of Norwich writes, "It is a very great pleasure to Christ when a simple soul comes to him nakedly, plainly, and unpretentiously."

To me one of the most moving moments during the Rite of Ordination is when the candidates prostrate themselves on the floor. A position of utter humility! Before God, before the Church, they are powerless, helpless, empty, for only in such a one can God's grace take root. To use that humble posture in prayer periodically is not a bad idea.

I once heard Archbishop Emory Kabongo, formerly a private secretary to Pope John Paul II, tell about a 3:00 a.m. phone call to the apostolic apartments from the Cardinal-Secretary of State to advise the Holy Father of an international emergency.

Archbishop Kabongo called the pontiff's bedroom — no answer. Worried, he went to the bedroom, knocked, entered — no pope. He glanced in the chapel — no sign of him. He checked the kitchen, dining room, private library — still no sign. He went up to the rooftop walking garden — no one was there. He retraced all his steps, this time looking more carefully, and, in the chapel, found Pope John Paul II prostrate, on the floor, praying.

A second aid to the development of humility: regular, sincere confession. The former bishop of Springfield, Illinois, Joseph A. McNicholas, once said at a day of recollection to priests: "If you are faithful to an honest, humble confession, at least once a month, you'll be a good priest." At the time I thought that was simplistic, but now I see it more and more as true not just for priests but for all of God's people. Worthy, integral, regular confession is itself an act of humility as we articulate with utter candor our sins; and what a source of grace and virtue it is as well!

Third is an openness to criticism. They say former President Lyndon Johnson always appointed one member of his staff to meet with him weekly to tell him bad news and to criticize him and his presidency. Johnson warned him that if he was too soft he would fire him. Bravo! Openness to criticism is a real boost to humility. From confessors, spiritual directors, our friends, our coworkers, our supervisors, we welcome criticism.

The sign of a true friend is one who is confident enough of the strength of the relationship that he can tell you things about yourself you need to hear, but perhaps would rather not.

None of us likes to hear criticism or bad news about ourselves, because we're proud. But an openness to criticism is a great help to humility.

"Who is free from defects?" asks St. Bernard. "He lacks everything who thinks he lacks nothing."

And if you would be truly humble, you must know yourself! Once when someone complimented St. John Vianney on being a good confessor, he said, "If I'm a good confessor it's only because I am a great sinner!" Humility means we know ourselves well; we are so cognizant of our weakness that we never place ourselves in occasions that we know can lead to sin.

A priest I know and love and respect, who had great influence on my vocation, invited me to go with him for a vacation to Las Vegas. He enjoyed golf, the shows, even a little blackjack. About two weeks before the trip I had to back out because the other assistant had emergency surgery scheduled. When I called to tell him I couldn't go, he was disappointed, and I said, "Well, you can still go by yourself, can't you?"

I'll never forget his reply: "I would never trust myself alone in Vegas."

This man, who was the model of priestly virtue, knew himself so well he would not put himself in an occasion of sin. Now that's humility.

You have heard of Matt Talbot, the great Irish layman: an alcoholic at twelve, through prayer, penance, and self-knowledge, he attained sobriety and remarkable sanctity. When he would walk home from the factory every night, he would cross the street rather than pass in front of a pub, knowing himself so well that he humbly admitted that even the smell or the sounds of the pub could tempt him severely. Now that's the kind of self-knowledge upon which humility grows.

"How can we feel our need of his help, or our dependence on him, or our debt to him, or the nature of his gift to us, unless we know ourselves?" asks Cardinal John Newman.

Humility, the favorite virtue of Our Lord, the cornerstone of growth in God's life: there are obstacles to it, there are helps to it; there are no replacements for it.

Let us pray the Litany of Humility of Cardinal Raphael Merry del Val:

> O Jesus! meek and humble of heart,
> Hear me.
> From the desire of being esteemed,
> Deliver me, Jesus.
> From the desire of being loved,
> Deliver me, Jesus.
> From the desire of being extolled,
> Deliver me, Jesus.
> From the desire of being honored,
> Deliver me, Jesus.
> From the desire of being praised,
> Deliver me, Jesus.
> From the desire of being preferred to others,
> Deliver me, Jesus.
> From the desire of being consulted,
> Deliver me, Jesus.
> From the desire of being approved,
> Deliver me, Jesus.
> From the fear of being humiliated,
> Deliver me, Jesus.
> From the fear of being despised,

Deliver me, Jesus.
From the fear of suffering rebukes,
Deliver me, Jesus.
From the fear of being calumniated,
Deliver me, Jesus.
From the fear of being forgotten,
Deliver me, Jesus.
From the fear of being ridiculed,
Deliver me, Jesus.
From the fear of being wronged,
Deliver me, Jesus.
From the fear of being suspected,
Deliver me, Jesus.
That others may be loved more than I,
Jesus, grant me the grace to desire it.
That others may be esteemed more than I,
Jesus, grant me the grace to desire it.
That in the opinion of the world, others may increase and
    that I may decrease,
Jesus, grant me the grace to desire it.
That others may be chosen and I set aside,
Jesus, grant me the grace to desire it.
That others may be praised and I unnoticed,
Jesus, grant me the grace to desire it.
That others may be preferred to me in everything,
Jesus, grant me the grace to desire it.
That others may become holier than I, provided that I
    become as holy as I should,
Jesus, grant me the grace to desire it.
Our Lady of Humility,
Pray for us.

When they had finished breakfast, Jesus said to Simon Peter, "Simon, son of John, do you love me more than these?" He said to him, "Yes, Lord; you know that I love you." He said to him, "Feed my lambs." A second time he said to him, "Simon, son of John, do you love me?" He said to him, "Yes, Lord; you know that I love you." He said to him, "Tend my sheep." He said to him the third time, "Simon, son of John, do you love me?" Peter was grieved because he said to him the third time, "Do you love me?" And he said to him, "Lord, you know everything; you know that I love you." Jesus said to him, "Feed my sheep."

— Jn. 21:15–17

CHAPTER 5

---✠---

Love and Chastity

$\mathcal{T}$he story is told of the Beloved Disciple, very advanced in years, near the end of his life in exile on the Isle of Patmos. There he lived in solitude in a cave surrounded by a few chosen disciples. Because he was the last of the Twelve, every Sunday hundreds of Christians would come to Patmos for the Eucharist and to see St. John. Sunday after Sunday the disciples would carry the frail apostle down to the crowd. When the time came for him to preach, the crowd would come closer, since his voice was barely above a whisper. Sunday after Sunday he would say the same thing: "Children, love one another! Children, love one another!"

Finally, after one such Sunday, one of his disciples, carrying him back to his cave, said, "Teacher, why do you keep repeating the same thing, over and over, 'Children, love one another'?"

"Because," replied the Beloved, "the Master kept repeating it over and over."

I want to reflect on love as the unifying principle that brings together and gives purpose to everything we do. Life is full of demands and expectations. The danger is that our lives can become disjointed, pulled in different directions, an engine off track. Thus, we look for a value to provide harmony, a principle to give unity, a force to give coherence, one motive to supply the direction under which everything we say and do can come — and that, I propose, is love.

St. Thérèse of Lisieux tells us in her autobiography that she had somewhat the same difficulty. The Little Flower recounts how she searched for an answer to her interior confusion, and she writes:

> I was not satisfied and could not find peace. I persevered... until I found this encouraging theme: "Set your desires on the greater gifts. And I will show you now the way which surpasses all others" (1 Cor. 12:31). For the Apostle insists that the greater gifts are nothing at all without love and that this same love is surely the best path leading to God. At length I had found peace! Love appeared to me to be the hinge for my vocation! I knew that the Church had a heart and that such a heart appeared to be aflame with love.... I saw and realized that love sets off the bounds of all vocations, that love is everything, that love embraces every time and place, that love is everlasting. Then, nearly ecstatic with joy, I proclaimed: O Jesus, my love, at last I have found my calling! My call is love. I have found my role in the Church.... In the heart of the Church I will be love!
>
> — OFFICE OF READINGS,
> FEAST OF ST. THÉRÈSE

Most of the time when we think of love we ponder our love for God and for his people. Natural enough — and important enough. First things first, though. The starting point of spiritual growth, the first step in true discipleship, is humble recognition of and profound gratitude for God's love for us. As the Beloved Disciple teaches, "In this the love of God was made manifest among us, that God sent his only Son into the world ... not that we loved God but that he loved us" (1 Jn. 4:9–10).

Those of you familiar with the Spiritual Exercises of St. Ignatius of Loyola know how he begins precisely with our recognition of God's gracious, undeserved love. One of our constant frustrations is accepting this deep insight that God passionately loves us. That's the "Good News," isn't it? The tragedy of life is that most of us feel it is just too good to be true, and go through life avoiding it or ignoring it. Many of us can echo that gripping passage from the *Confessions* of St. Augustine:

> I have learned to love you late, Beauty at once so ancient and so new. . . . You called me; You cried aloud to me; You broke my barrier of deafness; You shone upon me; Your radiance enveloped me; You put my blindness to flight; You shed your fragrance upon me. I drew breath and now I gasp at Your sweet odor. I tasted You, and now I hunger and thirst for You. You touched me, and I am inflamed with love of Your peace.
>
> — OFFICE OF READINGS,
> FEAST OF ST. AUGUSTINE

I remember a Jewish psychiatrist once saying to me, "Father, keep telling your people that God loves them. Most of the problems I deal with come from people who believe no one loves them, that they are unlovable, so therefore, they don't even love and respect themselves."

Every human being is loved by God and invited to love Him in response; particularly are those who believe in God's revelation in His Son called to be ever aware of His love and their duty to return it. To the point, however, the follower of Christ is called to have an intense awareness of the Lord's love for him, to accept it with humble gratitude, and to return that love with such intensity that he mirrors it to his people.

Now I ask you, how do we grow in our love of Christ and His Church? At the risk of oversimplification, I propose we "fall in love" with Christ and His Bride, the Church, in many of the same ways we grow in relationships of love and friendship on the natural level. I ask you, then, to remember present and past relationships of love and genuine friendship. Or, if you have never been in love with someone before, think of people close to you who have been, or simply ask yourself what steps you would take to grow in love with someone, or to strengthen and deepen a friendship.

To grow in our love with Jesus and His Church, would we not be expected to do certain things?

1. To grow in our love with someone, we first of all spend time with the other person. We converse with the other, we listen to the other, we enjoy being with the other.

The same is true in our love of Jesus, isn't it? We call being with the Lord — listening to Him and then conversing with Him — prayer. Thus, daily prayer is essential to our life, a *sine qua non.* Every day we find ourselves spending a chunk of time with our best friend, the Divine Lover, talking to Him, listening to Him. Prayer. We cannot grow in love with Jesus without it.

My mom and dad were very much in love. I heard others say they were like teenagers in their affection for each other, in the freshness and exuberance of their love. Dad left the house for work before 5:00 a.m., before any of us, even Mom, was up, but he always left a little note for Mom. At his coffee break he would call her; and when he returned home each evening at about 4:45, he and Mom would sit by themselves in the kitchen over a drink and spend an hour together. We kids just learned not to intrude. They sometimes chatted, sometimes said not much, sometimes engaged in rather animated discussion. Sometimes Mom would do the talking; sometimes Dad would. That daily time together, stealing quiet time by themselves, was the secret to their love.

The same is true in our relationship with Jesus. We must spend time alone with Him daily if our love for Him is to remain strong. The Liturgy of the Hours provides the perfect structure to pray daily with the Church from our rising to our going to rest at night. Personal prayer is essential. Some of us do this early in the morning; some late at night; some depend on Scripture; some prefer the holy-hour format; some call it meditation; some call it "centering." Whatever, however, whenever — if you want to fall in love with Jesus, and remain in love with Him, you must be with Him, talk with Him, and listen to Him every day. That is called prayer.

2. A way to enhance a friendship or relationship of love is to share a meal with the other. In our society, you know someone enjoys your company and wants to get to know you better when that person asks you out to eat. Well — again, pardon the over-simplification — we grow in our love for Jesus by often sharing the Eucharistic meal with Him. When we grow negligent, our love affair with the Master suffers. Likewise do we find ourselves savoring time before Our Lord really and truly present in the Bread of Life, the Blessed Sacrament. "He who eats my flesh and drinks my blood abides in me, and I in him" (Jn. 6:56). Pope St. Pius X wrote that the most effective way to grow in our love of Christ is to receive Him daily worthily in Holy Communion.

3. When we are in love with someone, we get to know that person's family and friends, don't we? You know a young couple's relationship is getting serious when they introduce each other to their families, when they begin to get to share one another's friends.

Well, we want Jesus and His Church to be the love of our lives. Get to know His family and friends!

Particularly is this true of His Mother. So close are we to Him that His Mother becomes our Mother. Thus has devotion to Our Lady become a standard of Christian spirituality. We need to recognize that there are different ways of loving Mary. How we love her is an open question; that we love her is not. A filial devotion to the Mother of Our Lord is likewise a definite part of our spirituality and a practical way to grow in our love of Jesus.

Nor do we neglect St. Joseph, John the Baptist — Jesus' family — and the apostles and disciples, His chosen friends.

A few years back when I was Rector at the North American College in Rome, I was approached by someone in a moment of particular trial, when he was questioning his entire relationship with Jesus and His Church. So burdened was he that he was on the brink of making what I considered a very rash decision. I urged him to at least give himself some time before he did anything final. The next day he returned much better, more confident of his love for Christ and His Church. What was the turning point? He told me he spent a few hours at the tomb of St. Peter, and concluded that if Jesus could love Peter, with all his flaws, sins, and mistakes, then Jesus could certainly love him! There's the power of getting to know the friends of Jesus so we can know and love Jesus even better.

All the saints, from Peter and Paul to the most recently beatified, are people we should strive to know and imitate— getting to know those friends of Christ is a practical way to grow in our love of Jesus himself.

But the people to whom we talk about Jesus don't have to all be saints! A lot of people are intimate with this man, Jesus, and they can help us develop deep bonds of unity with Him:

- We can turn to a spiritual director, someone wiser and more seasoned in his relationship with the Lord, who can encourage us in our love affair with Christ. This should set a pattern for our lives.

- The great ascetical writers have left us a legacy of spiritual reading to help us enhance our relationship with Christ. Thus, we enjoy reading St. Augustine, St. Francis de Sales, Thomas Merton, St. Teresa of Jesus, just to name a few.
- Our shepherds, the bishops, are close to Jesus (especially the Bishop of Rome) and guide us in their teaching office in our search for Christ and our love of the Church.

These friends of Jesus can help us become His friend as well.

4. When we want to grow in intimacy with someone, it is natural to try to discover everything we possibly can about that person. The same is true with Our Lord. "Theology," wrote Aquinas, "deserves to be called the highest wisdom, for everything is viewed in the light of the first cause."

The pursuit of theology — the study of God, the probing of Sacred Scripture, reading, reflecting, studying, discussing — is part of our growth in intimate love of Jesus, and makes no sense apart from that. Thus, studying is not a burden extraneous to our spiritual formation, but intrinsic to it.

One of the reasons the study of theology is essential is just that, when we love someone, we want to brag about the beloved, introduce others to the beloved, tell the whole world about him or her. That, as a matter of fact, is what we should spend our life doing — introducing the world to our beloved, Jesus the Lord. Well, we'd better know Him, understand His teachings, and be ready to defend Him with clarity, cogency, and compassion. And that's theology.

5. When we love someone, we desire to cleanse our lives of anything that could hurt our beloved. Thus, a basic characteristic

of our relationship with Our Lord will be a daily dying to sin and rising in virtue.

Thomas Merton describes the love of God as a brilliant ray of sunlight shining through a window. The light will always reveal streaks, or smudges, or dirt on the window. We let more light in the more we purify the window.

Thus, the way to receive more and more of the light of Christ's love is to constantly purify our life of sin. That is the exhortation found on almost every page of the Gospel — conversion, repentance, *metanoia* — call it what you want. The daily wrestling with that dark side of ourselves that holds us back from the freedom and self-giving that this romance with the Lord and His Church entails will be a constant of our friendship with Jesus.

There are practical ways to help us:

- Frequent examination of conscience as we forthrightly review our day, our week, as it compares with the commandments, the beatitudes, the virtues proper to our vocation. We praise God for growth and progress and seek His mercy and help with our sins.
- Openness with a spiritual director.
- The frank counsel of friends who are confident enough of their relationship with us that they can tell us areas of our life where we need to improve. One of life's greatest blessings is a friend who is not afraid to tell us the truth even when it is painful. And one of the greatest services we can provide a genuine friend is honestly letting him know of a concern we have about him. One of the toughest things I ever had to do was share with a friend that I felt a relationship in which he was engaged was threatening to compromise his celibate chastity. He told me to go to hell.

- If necessary, trust in a professional such as a psychologist or specialist who is trained in helping people deal with the hurts, hang-ups, or tendencies that hold them back from the freedom they need to love Jesus, His Church, His people.
- The correction we receive from others.
- And, very practically and powerfully, dependence upon the Sacrament of Penance. My first pastor always told married couples at the wedding, "The six most important words in a good marriage are 'I love you' and 'I am sorry'. Say those frequently and your love will be enduring."

It is in the Sacrament of Penance that we say to Christ and His Bride, the Church, "I am sorry." Thus, frequent celebration of this sacrament will characterize our love life with the Lord. While how often you approach the confessional should be a matter of discussion between you and your spiritual director, at least once a month seems a sound policy.

6. When we love someone we will die for that person. I once saw a little child bolt from its mother on a sidewalk and run out into a busy street. Without a moment's hesitation, the mother dashed out, completely oblivious to an oncoming truck. Thank God the truck stopped within inches of mother and child, but no one was surprised that the mother did that. True love prompts that willingness to die for the beloved.

If we wish to grow in our intimacy with Jesus, we must be willing not only to die *for* Him but to die *with* Him. Yes, the cross will be a part of our life. Why are we surprised when it comes? Why are we shocked when we suffer loneliness, frustration, failure, demanding people? Why are we tempted to think there is something wrong when sorrow and setback come? We are configured to the man on the cross, called to empty ourselves

perhaps to the point of death out of love for the crucified and
His Bride. He told us, "If you want to follow me you must deny
yourself and take up your cross." Will not a man endure hours of
dreary work daily for the woman and children he loves? So do we
followers of Christ endure weariness, stress, and agony for the
man and woman we love — Christ and His Church.

In my home parish, there was a wonderful couple who were
real pillars, happy parents of five children. She was crippled with
rheumatoid arthritis at thirty-four. It became such that she could
not leave her bed. He was so good to her — carrying her back
and forth, bathing her, keeping her company hours at a time,
feeding her. A few years ago I stopped to see them and, as we left
and walked out to the car, I said, "Bill, I am so inspired at how
tenderly you love Ginna."

"Father," he responded, "I love her more today than the day
I married her."

So our love for Jesus and His Bride, the Church, is most
proved in times of trial. In times of loneliness, rejection, suffering, tension — that's when love is pure. At times the man we
love, Jesus, might seem distant; at times His Bride, the Church,
might seem corrupt, mistaken, weak, scandalous — that's when
we love Jesus and the Church all the more! That's when love
proves itself!

The love we have for Jesus and His Church is not always a
carefree, pleasing, constantly satisfying, and fulfilling intimacy.
No — it will entail sacrifice, sweat, blood, tears, suffering; it will
entail the cross. At times, the cross will get to us, and we will
long to be free of it. Such is the weight of the cross that will reap-
pear consistently throughout our lives. Be ready for it!

Thus, to embrace the cross now through acts of self-denial,
mortification, and penance is a good way to deepen our love with
the crucified.

7. Finally, if we are trying to love someone, we learn to care for the people and activities he or she prefers. When two young people fall in love, for instance, she tries to learn something about baseball, he about art, so they can share interests. When we speak of Jesus, that interest means people in need and people who are poor in soul, mind, and body. This only comes from a heart that is sensitive to Christ.

"The love of Christ compels me," writes St. Paul. I don't know if I've succeeded, but what I have tried to do is demonstrate that our love of God — both the love God has for us and the love we return to Him — is the steam that makes the engine of our Christian life run, the principle that brings all the facets of our demanding life together. We exist because of love; hopefully, we are people who are so convinced of the Lord's gracious love for us that we love Him passionately in return, so intensely that we are configured to Him and share in the nuptial love Christ has for His Bride, the Church.

Everything we are about should strengthen, develop, nurture, and intensify this love: our daily prayer and reception of the Eucharist, our devotion to Our Lady and the saints, our dialog with our spiritual director, our study of God, our struggle with sin and growth in virtue, our willingness to sacrifice and suffer, and our service of His people. We do it all for love.

Perhaps you have heard of Catherine de Hueck Doherty, founder of the Friendship House Movement, whose cause for canonization has been introduced. She was once called to one of her famous houses that served the poor when it was experiencing internal strife. Staff members there were fighting and arguing, and she was called in to referee.

After listening to a couple of hours of bickering, she finally concluded the meeting and said, "I have reached a decision. I am closing this house!"

Well, shocked gasps went up all over. "But, Baroness, who will feed the poor and shelter the homeless?"

"The government can ladle soup and make a bed as efficiently as we can! We are called to do it with love, and if we can't do it with love, we're not doing it!"

We are called to be men and women who love and share that love with the people we serve, and if we cannot do it with love, there's no use doing it. All the knowledge about God and spiritual training in the world won't amount to a plate of gnocchi if we do not have love when we're doing it. You have seen Catholics who are people of love, who love Jesus and his Bride, the Church, passionately, and who radiate the joy, compassion, and conviction that flow from such a furnace of love. Most of us can trace our own faith back to a moment when we were blessed with such examples.

And you have seen Christians who have either never loved or have fallen out of love — cold, mean, crabby, petty, lazy, selfish. Oh, they love all right — they love themselves, not in the sense of self-respect spoken of by Jesus, but in a narcissistic, selfish way. Their convenience, their time, their career, their image, their wants — those things are supreme in this life for such people. The last thing the Church needs is "followers" of Christ who are like this.

In 1994, when I was at the North American College, we placed the statue of the Sacred Heart of Jesus at the entrance to our college. The Sacred Heart, burning with love and mercy for us, is a powerful symbol of the love Christ has for us. It is the unifying principle, the driving force of priestly life and for all followers of Christ; it is the only thing that gives sense, meaning, and purpose to everything we do.

>Sacred Heart of Jesus,
>I place all my trust in thee!

Sacred Heart of Jesus,
I believe in thy love for me!
Sacred Heart of Jesus,
May thy kingdom come!

———— ✠ ————

And the peace of God, which passes all understanding, will keep your hearts and your minds in Christ Jesus. Finally, brethren, whatever is true, whatever is honorable, whatever is just, whatever is pure, whatever is lovely, whatever is gracious, if there is any excellence, if there is anything worthy of praise, think about these things. What you have learned and received and heard and seen in me, do; and the God of peace will be with you.

— PHIL. 4:7–9

CHAPTER 6

——✛——

Human Formation

*G*race builds on nature," to use the legendary expression of St. Thomas. God's grace enhances, works through, and transforms our nature. We supply the raw material for God's amazing grace. A term I'm fond of using is "You can't make good gnocchi without good dough." I want to speak to you about the dough we supply for the Lord to work on. What is it in our personality, our character, our temperament that is supple to God's grace, that is clay in the hands of the Divine Sculptor, which He can use to bring people closer to Him? And what is it in our person, our nature that is resistant to His grace and could drive people away from Jesus and His Church? In other words, human formation.

When I was Rector of the North American College I would tell the seminarians, "As the seminarian, so the priest," as the adage goes. Most often we apply that to the supernatural life — if you pray and practice virtue as a seminarian, so you will as a priest; but if you don't, you won't as a priest either, because holy orders, while radically transforming your spiritual identity, will not alter your habits of life. Apply that to the human as well: if a seminarian is lazy he will be a lazy priest!

- A crab as a seminarian? Another crabby priest!
- A slob as a seminarian? A slob as a priest!
- Always late before ordination? You'll irritate people by not being on time as a priest.

- A shy seminarian who avoids people? Someone unlikely to do the aggressive evangelization the Church expects of her priests.
- Someone with b.o. or bad breath? A priest people will avoid.
- Someone who bores people silly with incessant chatter? People won't answer their doors when you come to visit.
- A gossip as a seminarian? So we will have another flannel-mouth priest!
- Someone who flies off the handle at the slightest thing? Another mean priest!

Because grace builds on nature, the Lord can only work with what we give Him.

The Church seems to be waking up to the value of human formation today. A few years ago I asked a bishop about a North American College alumnus; he sadly replied that the pastor had already asked to have him transferred. Why? I asked. A failure in preaching, in pastoral commitment, in theological preparation, in habits of prayer? None of the above! Why did the pastor ask to have the man transferred, then? Because his room was a pigsty! The housekeeper refused to go in. The man did not even flush his toilet. Now, that's not a supernatural problem, is it? That's about as human as you can get! Yet it debilitated this man's ability to function well as a priest. Human formation....

I asked a pastor about another alumnus. He rolled his eyes and shook his head. Again the litany of questions: Is it his preaching? No. His liturgical style? No. His lack of a prayer life? No. His inadequate theological foundation? Not at all. What's the problem, then? Answers the pastor, "The guy's just obnoxious." He elaborated that the guy was haughty, dismissive with the people, selfish with his time, arrogant with the staff, a know-it-all with the people. Again, human formation: nothing all that supernatural here, but a man whose manner, style, and personality drove people away instead of bringing them closer to Christ.

As Christians we are called to be bridge-builders, from *pontifex*, to use the local word. Our manner, our style, our personality is to attract people — not shock, scare, hurt, and alienate them. Thus must we be aware of those traits in our character that do indeed serve as a magnet to draw people to Jesus and His Church, and constantly enhance, refine, and improve them; and thus must we candidly confront those characteristics that wound, scatter, and scandalize people, and work to purge them from our temperament.

When Carl Mengeling was ordained bishop of Lansing, during his sermon he looked at Cardinal Maida, who was to consecrate him, and said, "Eminence, when it comes time for you to place the book of the gospels on my head, will you please press down real hard, because I've got to let that gospel penetrate through a thick, stubborn skull that very often resists the promptings of that gospel?" Don't we all? Sometimes we call this "evangelical effectiveness": in other words, what in my personality makes my living the Gospel smooth and effective, and what does not?

At the North American College, we stressed the spiritual and intellectual life. The seminary exists to provide an atmosphere where a student can grow intimately in love with Jesus and learn His Revelation with rigor and precision. I am proud that we got high marks in those two areas. Our men in general left there with a solid, disciplined, firmly rooted spiritual life and a fine theological education. But this doesn't help much if the human qualities are not as refined and attractive. What good will the prayer and learning be for the priest whose personality repels people? A man might know all about the theology of marriage, but, if he's so shy that he can't introduce himself to people, he won't have any young couples coming for marriage at all. A man's homiletic skills might be dazzling, but they won't do a bit of good if he yells at a crying baby from the pulpit.

Archbishop Fulton Sheen told the story about one of his first sermons as a priest in the parish. He had prepared it so well and polished it so much that he was sure it would go over. After the Mass he greeted the people and waited for some comment, but no one said a thing about his sermon. Finally, when all were gone, he asked the usher what he thought, and got the answer, "Frankly, Father, nobody could hear you." Now, knowing Fulton Sheen, I am confident that the content was marvelous . . . however, because of a simple human flaw — he spoke too softly — his sermon helped no one.

A man was golfing with his pastor and admired how the pastor sank every putt, while he himself was three- and four-putting every hole. He finally asked the pastor his secret. "Well, before every putt I say a 'Hail Mary.' " Next green, the pastor sank a long putt; the parishioner confidently said a "Hail Mary" and proceeded to miss the hole by three feet. The pastor looked at him and said, "Won't help you a damn bit if you don't know how to putt."

We have to know "how to putt" so that people are attracted to Jesus and His Church through us. Like it or not, our personalities can decide whether or not a person stays in the Church or not.

When I was a parish priest, I would visit fallen-away Catholics and I was surprised to find that, second only to irregular marriages, the major reason people left the Church was because a priest or nun had hurt them. "Oh, I was in the hospital and called and asked Father Smith to come see me and he never did." "My mother was dying and I asked Father Jones to bring her Holy Communion and he never did." "When my kids were going to school we fell behind in tuition and the pastor sent the kids home."

Those people left the Church because of a priest. Now, that's not logical, is it? To leave the Church because you do not like a priest is silly, and we know it. I remember as a child at my grandparents on a Sunday morning getting ready to go to Mass. My grandma said to my grandpa, "Come on, Tim, time to go to Mass."

He was comfortable in the easy chair reading the Sunday paper and replied, "I'm not going . . . I can't stand that new pastor."

To which my grandma responded, "Yeah, well, you can't stand the bartender up at the corner, either, but you sure as hell haven't quit going up there."

He got up and went to Mass.

Sure, it's silly to leave the Church because of the foibles of a priest, but many certainly do, and so all of us, clergy and laity, must be scrupulous in seeing that we never give anyone such an excuse. God forbid anyone should ever grow apart from Jesus and His Spouse, the Church, because of something we said or did, or something we did not say or do when we should have.

In 1996, I was at a reception at John Cabot University to celebrate the anniversary of the *New York Times,* when a well-known journalist came up to me. I had chatted with her in the past. This time she was very intense. She said to me, "Tell your men to be careful!" I asked what she meant, and she explained, "Rome can teach them a lot about what's good in the Church, but it can also teach them to be nasty, mean, ambitious, back-stabbing clerics." She went on to tell me that she had attended the big Mass in honor of newly beatified Edmund Rice at St.

Peter's on Monday, and when she left, it was pouring down rain. She had a deadline to meet and struggled to get a cab and had just found one — was actually opening the door to get in — when a priest pushed her aside and jumped in. She was furious. No telling how the nasty rudeness of that priest will affect her coverage of the Church in the future.

For better or worse, rightly or wrongly, all of us represent the Church to people. How people think of Jesus and His Church often depends on how we come across, how our human qualities are perceived. What a heavy responsibility! People can be driven away by us, and thus we must avoid not only any wrongdoing, but even the appearance of wrongdoing. On the other hand, people can be attracted to Our Lord and His Mystical Body through us — and what a joy that is!

Once on an airplane I sat next to a man who told me that he had converted to Catholicism because of the example of Cardinal Terence Cooke. I said, "Oh, yes, his patience and resignation during his agonizing death were so inspirational."

"Yes, they were," he replied, "but I had converted long before that. One day at an airport, there was a terribly long line to get the shuttle, and Cardinal Cooke was waiting in line in front of me. An attendant came up and whispered to him, 'Your Eminence, follow me. I will take you to the front of the line.' 'That's very thoughtful of you and I appreciate it, but I can wait my turn,' replied the cardinal. That act of simple humility moved me so much that it sparked my interest in becoming a Catholic."

We can bring 'em in; we can drive 'em away. Yes, the supernatural is essential, but we usually attract them or distract them by the human, natural side of our personality.

Now, let me mention three specific human qualities — and there could be dozens more — that people find particularly attractive in people.

The first is nebulous, I admit, but the only word I can use is "kindness." People love kind people. Cardinal John O'Connor of New York told the story that, shortly after he was ordained, he asked an older priest if he had any advice. The veteran said, "Why, yes, three pieces of advice: Be kind! Be kind! Be kind!"

Charles de Foucauld wrote, "To be an apostle, but how? With goodness and kindness, brotherly affection, a virtuous example. . . . Being patient as God is patient, being good as God is good, being a kind brother."

In one of Jon Hassler's novels, *North of Hope*, there is an episode where the struggling priest, Frank, was talking to the old pastor, Adrian, who had spent most of his life as chancellor of the diocese.

"I thought it was all so important then," says Monsignor Adrian, reflecting on his life in the chancery. "I thought the Church needed my talents as an administrator, and, maybe it did, but now that I'm a pastor again, I see what being a priest is all about. A man's talents are best put to use in parish work, Frank. And do you know what parish work consists of? What it comes down to? What our job really is?"

"What?" Frank asked.

"Being nice to people."

"That's all?"

"Loving kindness. Nothing more or less."

"Isn't that oversimplifying it, Adrian?"

"Nothing simple about it."

That's for sure. Being nice to people. There's nothing simple about it. Because I'm not talking about being some smiling childish airhead; I'm talking about a loving kindness that reflects the burning compassion of the Sacred Heart of Jesus. St. Francis de Sales, in his *Introduction to the Devout Life*, says we attract more souls with honey than with vinegar.

There's nothing simple about it, being kind. We are tempted to dismiss other people, to yell, to get fed up, to say we're too busy, to ask them how stupid they can be. Instead we are called to keep the smile, to let people think we've got all the time in the world for them, to exhibit a genuine interest, to ask about their families and remember their worries so we can inquire about them, to follow up on cases and get back to people . . . to be kind.

You want to know a few of the things that will appear unkind to people and that you should be aware of in your human formation?

Anger: never, ever, lose your temper and lash out at someone. One time while I was hearing confessions, I lost my temper and yelled at the penitent. She left the confessional — I'm sure in tears — in the middle of my tantrum. To this day I repent of that sin. To this day I pray for her. To this day I know that when I stand before the judgment seat of God that point will be brought before me.

I am not saying we are not to be firm, clear, and challenging with others. There are times we must be decisive, say no, state that certain behavior is unacceptable. A priest I know claims the great heresy today is "nice-ism," with priests and bishops so afraid of losing popularity or unsettling people that they turn into fluffy, least-common-denominator Christian ministers. That's not what I mean.

Yet, watch how you do it . . . and never act in anger and risk hurting someone.

Hurriedness: a second attitude that can appear unkind is seeming always to be on the run, busy, with no genuine time for others. They are then afraid to approach us because we give them the impression we have more important things to do.

Brusqueness: "I said 'good morning' to X and he didn't even look at me." The appearance of being aloof, unfriendly. Not that we all have to be backslapping, hail-fellow-well-met, campaigning-for-mayor type people.

Some of you are shy and always will be, but make sure people never interpret your shyness as a brusque unfriendliness. A cool, detached brusqueness detracts from the kindness people long for from others.

Be kind! Be kind! Be kind!

A second human trait that will enhance our evangelical effectiveness: reliability. People want to depend upon us.

- So, if we make an appointment, we keep it.
- If we promise to call someone, we do.
- If we are in charge of a particular parish organization, we make the meetings.

Reliability. People have a right to expect us to do what we're supposed to, to put in a good day's work.

I recently read a "letter to the editor" in *America* magazine from a parish priest in the Bronx, speaking about his ministry: "Once you're known, if you're available and approachable, if you believe the Gospel yourself, they'll be knocking at your door, dialing your number, and stopping you on the street. There's enough pain out there, enough anxiety, enough hunger for God to keep you busy all day, every day. How do you get known? You greet the people after Mass, you go into the school on a regular basis, you attend all the parish affairs, you visit shut-ins. Once you're known, if you're available and approachable, if you believe the Gospel yourself, you'll be busy."

A reliable availability to people means you are there for them. Recently I called a rectory at home and got a taped message: "Please call only during normal working hours, 9:00 to 1:00." Normal working hours? Normal for where? What's going on here? That's availability, with no emergency number to call? Does it not dawn on them that most people cannot approach a priest during "normal business hours," since most of them happen to be working?

Cultivate the human trait of reliability.

Start now! That's why a rhythm of life is so essential. If we are dependable, we get up at a certain time and go to bed at a certain time; we avoid late nights and late mornings; we have a faithful time for prayer, exercise, study, and fostering of friendships. And we get our work done. One of the highest goals of human formation is the development of a rhythm of life, from which reliability comes. We are people whose word can be trusted, who fulfill our duties, are immersed in our communities and present to those with whom we live — we are reliable.

A third human trait people look for: an upbeat, hopeful attitude. While such a posture must certainly flow from the supernatural virtue of hope, people are attracted to Christ and His Church through those who exhibit a sense of cheer and confidence, even in the midst of suffering, setback, and difficulty.

There are tendencies in all of us that militate against this upbeat, hopeful attitude people expect from us. One is a thin-skinned hypersensitivity that causes us to take offense at the least provocation. Some become easily aggrieved. They always think they're being cheated, overlooked, put upon. So they're always mad, upset, feeling sorry for themselves, and thus hardly exhibit the upbeat, hopeful character people crave.

We Christians can be a spoiled lot. While called to a life of selfless service, we are quick to insist on our rights, our prerogatives, and thus we often become petty. In 1996, something happened at the North American College to remind me of that. Three "crises" arose on the same day that upset me or other people in the house.

The first "crisis" came when I discovered that one of the workers at the school, who was preparing a mailing for bishops, had not used the formal "office of the rector" stationery. Next came the news from one of our candidates for diaconate that his retreat was "ruined" because they had been expected to wash dishes on retreat. Last, I found out that one of our men had rather rudely flicked the refectory lights on and off the night before, causing some of our visiting priests to become incensed. These were the three "crises."

I suppose I had a right to be upset (although not to become curt, which unfortunately I did!) over the oversight with the letterhead. The man to be ordained had a point that to wash dishes on a retreat was a distraction and imposition one hardly needs at a time of solitude and recollection. Our impatient student was perhaps legitimately put out that the priests were lingering while he was waiting for their dishes, and the priests had some cause for grievance that they were treated rudely by a student childishly flicking lights. But on reflection, I had to admit that the overwhelming majority of people in the world would welcome the day when such "crises" were all they had to worry about. All this was evidence to me of our tendency to become easily aggrieved.

This conviction was heightened that same afternoon, when Sister Virginia came to visit me. She was in Rome for a few weeks of break before returning to the mission school her order ran in Angola. She had photographs to excitedly show me of the sisters caring for very poor Africans, victims of plague, tribal violence, famine. She told me how the last time she returned to Angola, on the way home from the airport a band of thugs stopped the car, put a gun to each of the sisters' heads, and took all their belongings, chuckling about raping and murdering the sisters the whole time. Yet Sister Virginia was still eager to return to Angola; in the face of her upbeat, hopeful attitude, my three "crises" of stationery, dishwashing, and flicking lights quickly faded.

Mary, Queen of Scots, prayed: "Keep me, O God, from pettiness. Let us be large in thought, word, and deed. Let us be done with faultfinding and self-seeking. May we put away all pretense and meet each other without self-pity. And, O Lord, let us not forget to be kind."

I trust I've made my point. Notice that I have not spoken of anything particularly supernatural, of prayer, the spiritual life, orthodoxy, or faith — although such has to be the source of everything. No, I have spoken of human formation, the common, everyday traits we need to possess if we are to bring people closer to Christ by the goodness, power, and pleasantness of our personality, and the flaws and negatives that can drive people away.

A few final observations that can also help us:

Pray, of course. We ask the Creator who gave us our human nature to continue to mold it in the image of His Son. May I suggest especially two traditions that can help us every day to advance in human formation:

- One is the morning offering: each morning, immediately upon getting out of bed, we dedicate the entire day to God, and ask Him particularly for the graces we will need to attract people to Him by the goodness and appeal of our personality.
- Two, at the end of the day, we practice the habit of the examen: in the context of night prayer, we carefully review the day, particularly conscious of the times we may have hurt or offended people by a word, deed, or oversight, asking ourselves simply if we were that day a bridge for

people to reach God or a fence to place an obstacle. Daily honest examination of conscience keeps us sensitive about the presence or absence of human flaws.

Next, know yourself. Know yourself so well that you are gratefully aware of the traits in your personality that can attract people to Jesus, constantly trying to enhance those; and realistically aware of those flaws that periodically erupt and can drive people away, daily trying to refine and purge those away. Know yourself.

In your drive to know yourself, you will seek counsel from others whom you trust: a spiritual director, good friends, a pastor or supervisor, a counselor.

As I have said before, count as a genuine blessing the friendship of one who can tell you the truth about yourself, even when that hurts. A friend who is always telling you that you're just fine and that any criticism you receive from others is unfair is not a real friend.

A spiritual director helps one to develop the nature upon which God's grace builds. It is the spiritual director's duty to point out the areas of human formation where improvement is needed. None of us enjoys hearing about shortcomings. But, if evangelical effectiveness is a goal, if leading people closer to Jesus through the instrument of an attractive, pleasant, friendly personality is our drive, then we welcome such criticisms.

As we grow in self-knowledge with the help of prayer, counsel, and the direction of others, we find some things we cannot change, try as we might. I suppose we just keep trying and work on some other area of our humanity that we can improve. Some things we cannot change, even if people wanted us to. For instance, some people these days will reject what I say or do because I am a white, male Catholic Archbishop of European descent. Nothing I can do about that, is there?

Sometimes there are characteristics we have that damage our evangelical effectiveness, even though they should not. Sometimes people can be narrow or misguided in some judgments about us, but we should still be sensitive. For instance, I suppose people should not be turned off by a priest with a ponytail, a bushy beard, or an earring, but rightly or wrongly, they are, so a priest should avoid such things.

All I'm saying is that our personality, our human nature, our character, is one of God's greatest gifts to us. As he became incarnate in the human nature of His Son, so He becomes incarnate in our human nature. Thus our humanity can become a bridge, a door, a magnet drawing people to God and His Church. We constantly work to utilize those aspects of our humanity that attract people to salvation. And we ceaselessly try to cleanse from our humanity those dark, nasty, unpleasant traits that scare, shock, distract, or hurt people.

—✠—

Count it all joy, my brethren, when you meet various trials, for you know that the testing of your faith produces steadfastness. And let steadfastness have its full effect, that you may be perfect and complete, lacking in nothing.

— JAS. 1:2–4

CHAPTER 7

———✠———

Patience

"The virtue of patience is the one which most assures us of perfection," writes St. Francis de Sales in his classic *Introduction to the Devout Life.*

The famous "Bookmark of St. Teresa" comes to mind:

Let nothing disturb you,
Let nothing frighten you.
All things are passing.
God alone does not change.
Patience achieves everything.
Whoever has God lacks nothing.
God alone suffices.

Yes, "patience achieves everything." We could meditate on patience at any time, so essential is it to genuine discipleship. In his beautiful ode to charity, which he terms the foundational Christian trait, St. Cyprian concludes by observing, "Yet, take patience away from it . . . and it will not last! Take patience away, and it attempts to last without roots or strength."

It is a virtue central to the life of any authentic Christian, is it not? For that matter, it is necessary for success and happiness for any human being, even one without creed. All of humanity longs for it. It is perhaps the virtue that most escapes people, for all end up confessing, with a sigh, "Do I ever need more patience!" Everyone struggles for it. With customary candor the Little Flower wrote, "Restraining my impatience cost me so much that I was bathed in perspiration." Everyone extols the calm, patient person.

Yves Congar has a book entitled *The Need for Patience*, and at the start he describes it for us:

> Patience is a quality of mind — or, rather, of soul — which takes root in these profound existential convictions: first, that God deals the cards and fulfills in us his plan of grace; and second, that for great things, certain delays are necessary for maturation. . . . This profound patience is like the sower who knows the seed will grow. . . . Those who do not know how to suffer no longer know how to hope. The man who is too busy, and who wishes to enjoy immediately the object of his desire, does not know how to attain his goal. The patient sower who confides his seed to the ground and to the sun — he is the man of hope. . . .

Now, how to approach this pivotal virtue of patience? I propose we look at it in three ways: patience with God, patience with ourselves, and patience with others.

First, patience with the Lord. Are you startled that I contend we must work on being patient with God? Be honest: in our pride, do we not really at times think we know better than God? Do we not, in surveying the mess of His creation, sometimes observe that we could do a much more competent job of running the universe? Are we not tempted to run out of patience with Him and occasionally yell out, "This is no way to run a railroad"?

I remember a priest beginning a homily once at the funeral of a crib-death baby by saying, "All of us are tempted to say that God has made a terrible mistake." And are we not especially impatient with the Lord's apparent slowness in answering our prayers?

I recall once bringing Holy Communion to one of the housebound of the parish, a 90-year-old lady, right after the Berlin Wall fell, and asking her to pray for an increase in vocations. She responded, "Oh, hell, forget about that. I've been praying since I was seven for the conversion of Russia, and look how long it took Him to get around to that! I'm sure not going to be around another ninety years for Him to take his time answering another prayer!" Boy, I was sorry I asked! But yet was she not honest in expressing a very human impatience with the Lord, one we are all at times tempted to express?

Let's admit that we do become impatient with God in our prayer. The sterility, dryness, and tedium we experience in our prayer life lead us to a discouragement that tempts us to give up. We grow weary with the discipline, rhythm, and effort fruitful prayer requires, and we just get plumb tired of spending unending hours with nothing happening! We get impatient! Why in the name of God would He make something He so desires — our prayer — so difficult?

In his renowned *Life of St. Anthony*, St. Athanasius recounted an incident from the life of the great desert Father:

> Anthony entreated the vision that appeared, saying, "Where were you? Why did you not appear at the beginning, so that you could stop my distresses?" And a voice came to him: "I was here, Anthony, but I waited to watch your struggle. And now, since you persevered and were not defeated, I will be your helper forever."

Sorry, but that's the way God works in prayer. Father Wilfrid Faber wrote, "We must wait for God, long, meekly, in the wind and the wet, in the thunder and lightning, in the cold and the dark. Wait, and he will come. He never comes to those who do not wait."

The three essentials the Master himself taught for fruitful prayer are patience, perseverance, and persistence; so beware of that powerful temptation to become discouraged and impatient when our prayer is frustrating and dry.

Maybe that's why the older I get the more I come to appreciate and depend on two great prayers, the divine office and the rosary. Every day the priest patiently turns to his breviary. Some days, it is the only prayer, with his Mass, that he has time for; some days it is approached with less than the fervor it deserves; many times he is tempted to forget it. And yet, he patiently keeps at it, not only because he gave his word as a deacon that he would so pray daily with and for the Church in the liturgy of the hours, but because he patiently trusts that this prayer is efficacious, because through it he prays not alone, but with Christ and His Church.

And how I find myself more and more depending upon the rosary, patiently tolling away the beads, mind wandering, yes, to all the concerns and preoccupations that fill me up, but patiently joining Mary in pondering in my distracted heart the mysteries of the life, death, and resurrection of Jesus, the hinge of all history.

An article in *America* magazine some years back contained an interview with the Confessor of the Faith Archbishop Dominic Tang, imprisoned from 1958 to 1980 by the communists in China:

> Archbishop Tang laughed when I asked him how he spent his time for twenty-two years. "Everyone wants to know that. I prayed. You had to pray. You say the rosary,

counting the prayers on your fingers. You try to fill your mind with religious ideas. Otherwise, you are finished! In fact, after so many years, your memory becomes weak and you can't remember. But, everyone knows the rosary. You can say it easily. And saying the rosary includes repeating the whole life of Our Lord and the Blessed Mother...."

A patient prayer, the rosary is.

Then there is the impatience with the time it takes for God to answer our prayers. For Him, of course, "one day is like a thousand years," while we can hardly think past the next meal. St. Padre Pio says, "He has promised us that he will answer every prayer, but He has not told us how or when."

We are tempted to impatience with the Lord over our prayer... and we can also get upset with Him over the problem of evil.

The North American College in Rome, where I was rector, is right next door to the famous pediatric hospital Bambino Gesù. How often would I sit in the Blessed Sacrament Chapel praising God for His love and his goodness, only to have the solitude shattered by the sound of a little baby crying out in fear and pain next door at Bambino Gesù Hospital, and be tempted to say to the Lord, "Where is your love and goodness now?"

I was a priest only three months when I received a call in the middle of the night from the police. A woman in the parish was asking for me at the morgue to come identify the body of her husband. I had just baptized their first baby a few weeks before. The husband, out of work, had succumbed to depression, taken cocaine, driven to a dead-end road, stuffed the exhaust pipe with his undershirt, left the motor running, and sat in the closed car, taking his own life. She, understandably, could not bear to identify the body. I went... and then I tried to console her. When I returned I could not get to sleep. That young couple, that new family shattered, that little baby without a father, that young, fragile wife with no husband — how could I reconcile this with a loving God?

A situation like this can haunt us and lead us to impatience with a God who asks trust in the midst of such darkness. And get used to futility that can come when we simply have to say, "I don't know," when one of God's people angrily demands of us as Christians, "Why did your God let this happen?"

And, when we confront the evil and immorality of the world, the stubborn refusal of people to accept God's saving invitation, the blatant disregard for His law, the apathy and lethargy of people toward their faith, do we not grow impatient with God, and find ourselves like the apostles asking Him to rain down fire, or like the crowds begging for a sign to convince people? Yet, we have a God who prefers the gentle, soft, quiet way, who never imposes himself, who invites and then waits, who compares the growth of His reign to a tiny seed. We have a God who is eternally patient.

Now, as I am considering patience with God, may I talk about patience with the Church, since we believe the Lord is alive and active in His Church? I contend that we need patience with the Church. Some of us are impatient with the Church because we feel she is too slow, too plodding in renewal, too hesitant in keeping up with contemporary challenges, too cautious to take risks and leave behind outmoded discipline, doctrine, and devotion. Others are impatient with the Church for, in their view, being too quick to embrace new ideas, for abandoning her heritage and tradition, and for betraying the deposit of faith.

And yet the wise patiently trust her, conscious of her divinity and her humanity; like half of a faithful couple, loving the other whatever happens. Cardinal Newman said it well:

Trust the Church of God implicitly even when your natural judgment would take a different course from hers and would induce you to question her prudence or correctness. Recollect what a hard task the Church has; how she is sure to be criticized and spoken against, whatever she does; recollect how much she needs your loyal and tender devotion; recollect, too, how long is the experience gained in eighteen hundred years; and what a right she has to claim your assent to principles which have had so extended and triumphant trial. Thank her that she has kept the faith safe for so many generations and do your part in helping her to transmit it to generations after you.

Permit me a commercial here: the study of Church history gives you a great sense of patience with the Church. As Father John Tracy Ellis always said, "Simply put, Church history teaches you that she's been through it all before. You see the Mystical Body of Christ, warts and all, and you conclude that only an institution guided from above could have survived all of this." You know what Arnold Toynbee wrote in his *A Study of History:* "I believe that the Catholic Church is divine, and the proof of its divinity I take to be this: that no merely human institution, conducted with such knavish imbecility, would have lasted a fortnight!"

Mary Lee Settle, a novelist who won the National Book award in 1978, said that, when she became a Catholic, Walker Percy wrote her a letter of welcome and remarked, "It is a very untidy outfit you're hooking up with, but it's the one thing that will be around till the end."

We need to listen to what Pope John Paul II said to young people at the first World Youth Day:

I should like to ask you, dear young people, for a favor: be patient with the Church! The Church is always a community of weak and imperfect individuals. But God has placed his work of salvation in human hands. This is indeed a great risk but there is no other Church than the one founded by Christ. He wants us human beings to be his collaborators in the world and in the Church with all our deficiencies and shortcomings.

Enough of patience with the Lord, patience especially in our prayer, in confronting evil, and in loving His Bride, the Church. We also need patience with ourselves.

Listen again to St. Francis de Sales: "Be patient with everyone, but above all with yourself. I mean, do not be disturbed with your imperfections, and always rise up bravely from a fall." We want to be saints. We have heroes such as Jesus, St. Paul, the Curé of Ars, St. Francis of Assisi, Don Bosco, Maximilian Kolbe. All that said, we are then ripe for the temptation to become impatient with ourselves when we fail to measure up, as we almost always do!

Wisdom warns us that impatience with self leads to a discouragement that can deaden us. What is the answer? To lower our goals? No! The answer is to be as patient with ourselves as the Lord is with us, to realize His grace is more powerful than our weakness, and to admit that most of our life is patiently stumbling along with His help. So, the greatest tragedy is not in our falling, but in our not getting back up. Bishop Fulton Sheen says Jesus fell three times on the road to Golgotha because three represents infinity, and so there is no end to the number of times we may fall under the weight of our own crosses.

Now, let's be candid. We especially lose patience with ourselves in our struggle with inclinations to sin, especially to sins of the flesh. Satan is especially potent in convincing us that our struggle to remain pure is a losing battle undertaken only by fools, and that falls should convince us to quit trying. Thus, we lose patience in our battle with sin, be it a weakness of chastity, temper, laziness, drink, a malicious tongue — whatever. Don't listen to him!

As Evelyn Underhill writes, "Patience with ourselves means patience with a growing creature whom God has taken in hand and whose perfection he will complete in his own time and way." And what a vicious circle it becomes! We are trying so desperately to remain sinless, to grow in virtue, and the fall comes . . . the sharp word, the unchaste act, the temper tantrum, the unfair judgment . . . and we lose patience with ourselves, we get discouraged, we wander away from prayer and God's mercy, and sin becomes easier. Ask the recovering alcoholic about the morning after! So down on himself that the only answer is another drink! Can we not be as patient, as gentle, as hopeful, as respectful, as compassionate with ourselves as the Lord is with us?

Two helps in preserving patience with ourselves? Spiritual direction, where one whom we trust and who knows us well can keep us from impatience with ourselves, which leads to wallowing and discouragement; and the sacrament of penance, approached frequently, which effectively restores us to full friendship with Our Lord and cuts short the cycle of falling further.

The mystic Julian of Norwich recorded, "I was left to myself in depression, weary of my life and irked with myself, so that I kept the patience to keep going only with difficulty . . . but immediately after this Our Lord again gave me comfort and rest of soul in delight and certitude."

Patience with God, patience with ourselves . . . and finally, patience with others. Usually, of course, we approach it the other

way, and consider the virtue of patience to mean just with others. I trust you see my point. Odds are we will not be patient with
others if we are not patient with the Lord and patient with ourselves first.

Several years ago, the Archdiocese of New York lost Father
Brian Barrett — a great priest, a member of the seminary faculty,
an alumnus of the North American College — at the young age
of forty-two. After his sudden death, an interesting story sur-
faced about a woman journalist. Seems she was covering the
story of the papal visit to New York a year-and-a-half before and
was referred to Father Barrett for background in her research.
She described herself then as a radical feminist, an "ex-Catholic"
who detested the Church and believed it to be the incarnation
of everything she considered backward, repressive, unhealthy,
and unhappy. You know the type. She unloaded all the barrels on
Father Barrett.

How did he react? You know he had to be tempted to lose his
patience with her. Instead, he listened, calmly answered her questions, reasonably explained Church teaching, put up with what
she admitted in retrospect were insults and taunts, kept meeting
with her, and never lost his cool. The result? She was in tears at
his funeral; she has returned to the Church; she now cherishes her
faith and loves her religion. He may have been tempted to lob a
grenade; instead, he cast a fishing line, patiently reeled her in ...
and it worked. A soul has been healed and saved.

Now, no doubt about it, you are going to meet people who
could prompt people like the late Mother Teresa to lose her
cool! You bet you will at times have to be very firm, to correct
abuses, to speak up to preserve the truth, your self-respect, and
your peace of mind. All I'm saying is that it is always more laudable, preferable, and more effective if we do so calmly, reasonably,
and patiently.

What helps us maintain our patience with others?

Humility helps: pride, you see, leads to impatience because it tempts us to think we know best and have all the answers. Humility helps us admit that we are but an instrument. You remember the night prayer of Pope John XXIII: "Well, I did the best I could. . . . It's your Church, Lord! I'm going to bed. Good night."

A sense of humor helps us keep patience with others. It's interesting that, in the St. Thomas' presentation of the virtues, the virtue of patience comes under hope, as does the virtue of joy. If we trust that all is in God's hands, well, it will work out in God's good time, so we might as well patiently work and learn to laugh. Maybe our plans are not the right ones anyway. Listen to this jingle of Father Solanus Casey, the Detroit Capuchin who, God willing, might soon be beatified:

> We cook up plans but turn ill
> with too much flavoring of self-will.
> If this idea comes from heaven
> it will grow like leaven.
> God demands to use our powers
> if we don't spoil his plan with ours.

Another help? Interpreting slights, inconveniences, and less-than-perfect situations as occasions of grace and opportunities to grow in virtue. St. Rose of Lima said, "Without the burdens of afflictions it is impossible to reach the height of grace. The gifts of grace increase as the struggles increase."

A healthy sense of original sin. Do we not believe that there is a fatal flaw in creation, that something is wrong, that, as St. Paul says, "All of creation groans in agony"? Sometimes we get impatient because we expect perfection. I remember two years after I was ordained being elected to the priests' personnel board. At my first meeting on the agenda was the case of a young priest who was asking to be moved after his second very tense assignment with a very trying pastor. I spoke up: "What this priest needs now is to be assigned to a warm, loving, wise, holy pastor." Six pairs of eyes glazed over and six jaws dropped. Finally Archbishop John May broke the silence and remarked, "And where in the hell are we going to find him?" Why are we surprised that any situation in which we find ourselves is imperfect, less than ideal, flawed?

Another aid to patience with others? A talent for communication. You see, to remain patient, we must be able to let people know when we are hurt, or disappointed, or upset about something. For, if we do not, it will only fester and erupt. The skill comes in communicating calmly, reasonably, nonjudgmentally, a talent that we are always developing.

And, of course, a childlike trust in God's providence. "We know," St. Paul writes to the Romans, "that in everything God works for good with those who love him, who are called according to his purpose." His plan will ultimately prevail; He has conquered; He is Lord! How can we be anything but patient with the people and with the situations we are in?

Charles de Foucauld asked, "To be an apostle, yes, but how? To some, without ever saying to them anything about God, being patient as God is patient, being good as God is good." The greatest example of and inspiration for patience is the cross of Christ.

I used to bring Holy Communion to a man by the name of Charlie Marsh. He had suffered a paralyzing stroke at a young age. People told me he had been a handsome, vigorous, active, athletic man with the world by the tail when he was felled by the stroke. I used to be amazed at his tranquility, his patience in suffering, his smile. He could only communicate by blinking. One

Friday, though, as I stood near him, I noticed he was perplexed, blinking rapidly, his usual composure and smile gone. I summoned Teresa, his wife, who said, "Oh, Father, please move aside a bit. Charlie always likes to look at the crucifix on the wall, and you are blocking his view."

So that explained the smile, the peace, the patient resignation. His unimaginable sufferings were united with those of Jesus on the cross; he garnered inner strength and patience from the example of Our Lord's patient endurance. Should not we all be configured to Our Lord who offered himself on the cross?

Many of us — especially members of Alcoholics Anonymous — know by heart the opening words of Reinhold Niebuhr's famous prayer. But listen to it as a fitting prayer on patience:

> God, give us grace to accept with serenity
> the things that cannot be changed,
> courage to change the things
> which should be changed,
> and the wisdom to distinguish
> the one from the other.
> Living one day at a time,
> Enjoying one moment at a time,
> Accepting hardship as a pathway to peace,
> Taking, as Jesus did,
> This sinful world as it is,
> Not as I would have it,
> Trusting that You will make all things right,
> If I surrender to Your will,
> So that I may be reasonably happy in this life,
> And supremely happy with You forever in the next.
> Amen.

———✠———

"Yet even now," says the LORD, "return to me with all your heart, with fasting, with weeping, and with mourning; and rend your hearts and not your garments." Return to the LORD, your God, for he is gracious and merciful, slow to anger, and abounding in steadfast love, and repents of evil.

— JOEL 2:12–13

CHAPTER 8

———✠———

Penance

The name of Gene Hamilton may be new to you if you are not from the Archdiocese of New York or have not read *A Priest Forever* by Father Benedict Groeschel (published by Our Sunday Visitor in 1998). Gene was a seminarian for that archdiocese at St. Joseph's Seminary, Dunwoodie. From all accounts, he was a fine student, a friendly, sincere young man, eager to be a priest. He was diagnosed with cancer, and the final years of his life were a real cross for him — pain, decline, hopes way up after surgery and treatment, only to have them dashed with another outbreak. In his brave struggle a saint emerged, and I use that word purposefully.

In his pain, agony, and dwindling strength, a man of deep faith, indomitable hope, and genuine love arose; a seminarian of prayer, who never complained, thought more of the needs and difficulties of others than his own. A man driven by one desire: to be united with Jesus in His passion and death, hopefully, yearning to do so as a priest. There was a lot of longing for a miracle by his family, brother seminarians, friends and admirers; many, including doctors and other medical personnel, told the young man, "You're going to beat this, Gene." Dozens who just knew he was too good, too innocent, too pure and holy to die so young and painfully, prayed for his recovery.

In January of 1997, Gene Hamilton was too ill to come on the pilgrimage to Rome with the other men from Dunwoodie, the seminary he was attending. Bishop Edwin O'Brien, with the late Cardinal John O'Connor, approached the prefect of the Congregation for Catholic Education, the dicastery of the Holy See under which seminaries come, for permission to ordain Gene Hamilton should he worsen, and received the proper dispensation. Upon his return to New York, Bishop O'Brien visited him in the hospital, and, having been briefed on his condition, with Cardinal O'Connor's approval, ordained him a deacon and a priest on his hospital bed. Two hours later, Father Gene Hamilton died, at twenty-four years of age.

His long struggle and his dying have moved many people. Dozens have told stories of his patience in suffering, his closeness to the cross of Christ, his enduring conviction that all that really mattered was "Christ, and him crucified." Apparently, during his stays in the hospital, he would pray a lot. One of his favorite devotions was the Stations of the Cross. At the end, without the strength to reach the chapel, he would shuffle down the corridor of the hospital, dragging his IV and oxygen, and stop at fourteen different hospital rooms, designating each of them one of the stations, recognizing in each cancer patient the suffering, bleeding Savior on the *via crucis*. To Gene Hamilton, his life had meaning, purpose — his suffering was salvific — if united with the passion and death of Jesus. And the sentiment of the Church of New York is that this priest of two hours, so configured to Christ on the cross in life, is now indeed a sharer in his resurrection.

To be in union with Jesus in His dying so we can join him in His rising. . . . Jesus and His Church expect everyone to be like Father Gene Hamilton, configured to Jesus in His passion and death. The virtue of penance is essential in the life of every genuine disciple.

The virtue of penance . . . call it self-denial, mortification, self-abnegation . . . it means curbing, taming, controlling, dying to the cravings, comforts, lusts, longings, and appetites of the flesh, of this world, to live more freely and intimately with Jesus. It is not a popular virtue today, this one of penance. But, then, it never has been. As Thomas à Kempis wrote in his *Imitation of Christ* centuries ago:

> Jesus has always had many who love his heavenly kingdom, but few who bear his cross. He has many who desire consolation, but few who care for trial. He finds many to share his table, but few to take part in his fasting. All desire to be happy with him, few wish to suffer anything for him. Many follow him to the breaking of the bread, but few to drinking the chalice of his passion. Many revere his miracles, few the cross.

Penance has never been popular, but especially not today. The historian in me wants to figure out why this age thinks itself exempt from the call to self-denial and mortification. Is it the loss of the sense of sin, which would, of course, render self-abnegation superfluous, since one of the reasons we practice penance is in reparation for our sins? Is it the New Age thinking that sees every human desire and urge as basically good and deserving to be satisfied? Is it due to the bogeymen of secularism and materialism? Is it just raw hedonism? It could be a loss of the sense of the supernatural, since people today are frantically practicing self-denial through fasting and painful exercise for the earthly benefit of good health. I don't know all the reasons why this age belittles the spiritual value of penance. I don't really care, since none of them amount to a hill of polenta, because haunting us always are the words of the only person who really makes a difference:

"Unless you do penance you shall perish!"

"Unless you take up your cross and follow me you cannot be my disciple!"

As the Holy Father preached a few years ago on Ash
Wednesday: "When we forget the need for penance, self-denial,
and sacrifice, we forget the fact of our sinfulness. When we forget we are sinners, we forget our need for Christ. And when we
forget we need Christ, we have lost everything!"

It seems to me that penance can come in three ways:

- One, as we voluntarily take upon ourselves practices of
  mortification.
- Two, as we accept the rejection that necessarily comes
  from the world when we are loyal to the Gospel.
- Three, when we gracefully embrace the adversities and
  sorrows that just plain come with life.

I want to elaborate on each of these three avenues of
penance.

We conform ourselves to the passion and death of Jesus by
freely taking upon ourselves acts of self-denial. This is the mode
of penance most associated with Lent, as we voluntarily give up
certain food, drink, smoking, entertainment, or legitimate pleasure, or take upon ourselves a practice we find difficult, such as
rising earlier or walking when we could ride.

It is especially this first kind of penance that has today
declined in popularity. Those of you older can remember when
this kind of penance was legislated by Church discipline, result-
ing, for instance, in mandatory Friday abstinence all year and
required fasting every day of Lent. The canonical requirement is
gone, a move that was meant to purify our motives but not elim-

inate voluntary penance. Unfortunately, the baby went out with the bath water.

Be that as it may, it is safe to say that voluntary acts of self-denial are a singularly effective way of growth in holiness. It would be difficult to find any saint who did not have specific practices of mortification as part of his or her spiritual regimen. I remember being very moved when I read in a biography of Pope Paul VI that he wore a hair shirt as an act of penance. Anyway, we can conclude that acts of voluntary self-denial must be a part of everyone's life.

Why are acts of self-denial effective in our spiritual growth? The ascetical theologians give us some answers. For one, acts of mortification allow us to feel closer to the passion of Christ. The temporary, passing discomfort caused by denying ourselves a legitimate comfort or pleasure reminds us of the love of Jesus exemplified most dramatically in the supreme act of voluntary self-immolation, the cross. Two, giving something up usually creates a vacuum in our lives, an emptiness which then, so the ancient wisdom goes, can be filled by the Lord. Three, denying ourselves a legitimate pleasure trains us to deny the illegitimate ones. If I can curb my appetite for ice cream, for instance, well, then, maybe I can curb my tongue when I am tempted to say something unkind. In other words, we train ourselves to say no to acceptable comfort and pleasure so we can then, with the grace of God, say no to the temptations to sin that come along.

It is a rather practical, effective, simple wisdom here, one backed up by Scripture, Tradition, and the example of Jesus, who himself fasted. May I mention three special areas where voluntary acts of self-denial are particularly appropriate?

1. The sacrifice of time. It would be difficult to find a commodity more precious to us than time, and a penance we must always embrace is to sacrifice time.

Time with the Lord in prayer! Henri Nouwen once defined prayer as "wasting time with the Lord." How sacrificial for us, pragmatic that we are, to mortify ourselves by giving the Lord the time He deserves in prayer. I remember the first time I made an eight-day Ignatian retreat. The first day I had a real problem persevering through my four assigned hours of meditation. I reported that fact to my director the next day, reasoning that I needed to be practical and thus should trim the hour to forty-five minutes. Whereupon he prescribed four one-hour-and-fifteen-minute periods of prayer for that day, informing me that St. Ignatius insisted that we add to the hour the time we are tempted to cut. Needless to say, I did not complain again!

Fidelity to daily prayer, even when nothing seems to be happening, can be a real sacrifice of time, but one most appropriate for us. We all occasionally find ourselves wondering if the batteries in our watch have gone out as we periodically struggle through our set time for prayer. That is an act of penance most fitting for us, sacrificing time, "wasting time with the Lord" in prayer.

We also sacrifice time for others. The demands made on our time! How we long for an evening alone, an afternoon without the phone or doorbell interrupting us, a day without appointments. Again, we are asked to sacrifice our time, freely to give up something we find precious. Woody Allen said "half of life is just showing up," and that's very true for all of us. It calls for a real sacrifice of time, which can be a penance.

2. A second style of voluntary penance that is most called for is simplicity of life. I propose to you that a genuine simplicity of life entails voluntary self-denial, because it is very natural for us to become sated, comfortable, cozy, and just plain spoiled. Thus, to learn to deny ourselves some comforts, possessions, and perks to protect our evangelical simplicity is an essential lesson.

3. A third area of freely undertaken penance most appropriate comes in our ongoing struggle with our dark, unredeemed side. As Fulton Sheen said, "A saint is only a recovering sinner." The wise person is acutely aware of his weaknesses, his inclination to sin, his dark side. All of us, redeemed though we are, have evil spirits lurking within, and the first step in victory over them is identifying them, owning up to them. Our life then becomes a constant struggle to keep them in check, to make sure that only Jesus, and no one or nothing else, has dominion over us. The sacrifice comes because that is hard work! We can never let up in our vigilance and self-control! The minute we think we're strong and have mastered our sinful nature, we're setting ourselves up for a fall.

What will lurk deep within you for the rest of your life? Laziness, a temper, lust, a desire for recognition and prestige, a longing to control, anger, a sharp tongue, drink, gluttony? We all have one, or two, or three of these unsettling, dangerous spirits. To control them, moderate them, keep them in check, is a life-long struggle that demands sacrifice.

I remember once in my college seminary days, Cardinal John Carberry, the archbishop of St. Louis, came to talk with us about the priesthood. Now, Cardinal Carberry was one of the most pious, saintly gentlemen you would ever want to meet. After his talk, he invited questions, and one of the guys said, "Yeah, Your Eminence, when does the priest stop having bad thoughts and temptations against purity?" Well, there was a gasp from all of us! This was just not the kind of question one should address to the cardinal! But, without missing a beat, the cardinal responded, "Oh, about five minutes after you're pronounced dead." This pious man knew well that the struggle with sin never lets up! And it cannot be won without self-denial.

Now, before I conclude this consideration of voluntary penance, let me mention a few caveats:

1. While some freely embraced mortification is essential for all of us, it is always wise to discuss it with a spiritual director. We can at times get excessive in our penance. If our voluntary acts of mortification harm our health, sap our energy, or make us crabs, they are counterproductive.

2. Be careful of pride! Sometimes voluntary penance can be counterproductive when we start congratulating ourselves for being so heroic for God. If our freely embraced acts of mortification attract attention to ourselves, they are counterproductive. As St. Padre Pio said, "Self-denial is not our gift to God, but allowing God to do more for us!"

3. In our Catholic tradition, voluntary penance is particularly beneficial when it leads to charity for the poor, acts of mercy to those in need. As St. Peter Chrysologus said: "When you fast, if your mercy is thin your harvest will be thin; when you fast, what you pour out in mercy overflows into your barn. . . . Give to the poor, and you give to yourself. You will not be allowed to keep what you have refused to give to others."

We are called to penance by gracefully accepting the difficulties and opposition that come from our loyalty to the Gospel.

The Eternal City is filled with examples of men and women who excelled in this kind of self-sacrifice. We call them martyrs. They gave their lives simply because their convictions clashed with the prevailing values.

In 1997 when I was at home in the United States, I spent time with Cardinal John O'Connor. One of the priests closely associated with him told me that, in spite of the cardinal's protests, the New York Police Department regularly has two plainclothes officers near him at each public appearance because of the multiple threats on his life. Think of the burden the late cardinal had to be under because of that hostility. Why? Because of his ardent defense of the unborn and his perceptive questioning of the militant homosexual lobby.

Or consider the late Cardinal Joseph Bernardin, who bore the heavy cross of vicious, scurrilous accusations, fed, it now turns out, by a priest who detested him because of what he called his "liberal policies." That's what I'm talking about: two brave men who faced harassment and persecution because of their loyalty to the Gospel of Christ. Now, this was not voluntary penance, because neither had asked for it. This type of mortification had come to them simply as a result of their principles.

And so will this kind of penance come to anyone worth his salt. If we do not unite this with the supreme persecution and rejection that Jesus experienced during His passion, it will wear us down. Remember the eloquent quote of Pope Paul VI: "When it is hard to be a Christian, it is easy to be a Christian. And when it is easy to be a Christian, it is hard to be a Christian." We are often tempted to interpret rejection and opposition as signs of failure, whereas in the dispensation of Christian paradox they are proofs of the authenticity of our discipleship. When we face slings and arrows because of our fidelity to Christ, we share in His cross. Remember what St. Thomas said, that the greatest lesson of the cross is that Jesus could have avoided it, but instead freely embraced it to demonstrate dramatically the intensity of God's love and the horror of sin.

We, too, can escape the cross, and sink into a bland, comfortable, feel-good state of existence. As Thomas Reeves, a biographer of John F. Kennedy, wrote in the October, 1996, edition of *First Things*:

> Christianity in modern America is, in large part, innocuous. It tends to be easy, upbeat, convenient, and compatible. It does not require self-sacrifice, discipline,

humility, an otherworldly outlook, a zeal for souls, a fear as well as love of God. There is little guilt and no punishment, and the payoff in heaven is virtually certain. The faith has been overwhelmed by the culture, producing what is rightly called cultural Christianity.

Well, sorry, but, as much of a cliché as it has become, we are called to be countercultural, and as most of us learned on the playgrounds in first grade, when you oppose the in-crowd, you'd better be prepared to be ignored, ridiculed, and knocked down. G. K. Chesterton said that "Christianity not only comforts the afflicted but afflicts the comfortable." I am afraid that the world still apes those who taunted Jesus to "come down off the cross," for they much prefer a religion of ease, affirmation, agreement, and soothing. We are called upon to be countercultural because:

- to a society of violence and revenge, we stand for peace and forgiveness;
- to a world sated with sex, we are modest and chaste;
- to a society frantic to spend, own, and hoard, we model simplicity and sharing;
- to a country that blames and scorns the poor, we urge care and justice.

And that will cost us in terms of popularity, prestige, and power; and this, I contend, makes sense only if we interpret it as penance, as a chance to conform ourselves to the rejected, scorned, persecuted Savior.

A life of loving service to Christ and his Church in obedience is a freeing, creative promise. But we are really naïve if we do not think obedience to Our Lord's teachings will at times require dying to self.

All I am saying is that penance will come necessarily if we are true to a life of fidelity to Our Lord, His teaching, and His Church. Be ready for some pain, rejection, and mortification. Maybe not a "red" martyrdom, but certainly a "white" one. It only makes sense if we unite it all to the passion of Our Lord.

Finally, penance enters our lives as we gracefully embrace the adversities that just plain come with life. As C. S. Lewis wrote, "Christianity does not take hardship from life; it simply gives one a reason to endure it." Father Gene Hamilton did not voluntarily ask for his fatal cancer, did he? Nor did it come to him as a result of his fidelity to the Gospel, did it? His cross came like most do — because tears, sorrow, sickness, and adversity come with life. And the virtue of penance is an invitation to give them meaning, make them redemptive, by interpreting them as opportunities to conform ourselves to our suffering Savior.

Aleksandr Solzhenitsyn observed that the great heresy of modernity is to believe that progress, prosperity, health, and happiness are the ordinary, expected conditions of life, and that, thus, frustration, boredom, sickness, pain, setbacks, and struggles are flaws, failures, and glitches that must be avoided and from which we must escape at all costs. And yet, we have a Master who says, "He who loves his life will lose it; he who loses it for my sake preserves it to eternity."

Life is jammed with frustrations and heartaches. One of the greatest blessings of the Gospel is that it provides a reason to bear them joyfully and achieve life and happiness through them.

Every one of you carries a dozen crosses a day, some heavy, some trivial. All those crosses come naturally just because you get out of bed each morning — which, by the way, is usually the first cross of the day.

The cross is there! We cannot get away from it! And in every one of those we hear the whisper of Christ, "Take up your cross and follow me!" This is penance in its purest form! Every single one of us is invited daily to embrace the cross. Listen to St. Francis de Sales:

> The everlasting God has in his wisdom foreseen from eternity the cross that he now presents to you as a gift from his inmost heart. This cross he now sends you he has considered with his all-knowing eyes, understood with his divine mind, tested with his wise justice, warmed with loving arms, and weighed with his own hands to see that it be not one inch too large and not one ounce too heavy for you. He has blessed it with his holy Name, anointed it with his grace, perfumed it with his consolation, taken one last glance at you and your courage, and then sent it to you from heaven, a special greeting from God to you, an alms of the all-merciful love of God.

Let me mention a few of the more predictable crosses that come to us, not because we ask for them, but just because we get out of bed each morning and want to be decent people.

One is the penance of listening. A wise priest I know back home says that listening is the full-time job of a priest, listening to the Lord, listening to his people. "Ministry of ears," it is sometimes called.

I remember being in a parish only a couple of days when a woman called up and asked to see me. When I entered the parlor and introduced myself, that was the last word I said. For a solid hour she talked, cried, talked some more, and then got up and said, "Thank you, Father, I am much better!" I had not said a word!

To listen with attention, sensitivity, and interest is a skill — and can be a penance. Learn it. Do you listen attentively, looking at people, interested in what they say? Or are you a chatterbox, self-absorbed, bored with the conversation of others, preparing your next response? Listening is a wonderful skill — and takes mortification.

Then there is "goodness fatigue." Ever hear of that? We just plain get tired of doing good! Dorothy Day claims that one of the most important lines of Scripture is: "Brethren, do not be weary in well-doing" (2 Thess. 3:13). Daily do we battle sin, vice, evil, Satan, selfishness, sickness, and it takes its toll. At times we just get weary of doing good. St. Mark says, "Jesus went about doing good," and so do his people. But doing good constantly is hard work, a daily cross. We want to run and hide, turn off the phone, lock the door, have a couple of drinks, spend the day in bed, become a cable TV junkie, tell people we're sick of their whining . . . but daily are we called to do good, and that can be a cross.

The "blahs" can be another daily mortification. Yes, a Christian's life can be one of the most exciting, interesting, challenging ways of life around, but there can be tedium and boredom. There's a lot of things that can get to us, making us ask after a while why we do what we do. Unless we daily accept these doses of the "blahs," again, as an invitation to persevere with Christ on the road to Calvary, the "blahs" can ruin us.

Finally, a penance you will find in everyone's life: the daily cross of just doing well the ordinary, routine duties of life for the glory of God and love of his people.

At the celebration in honor of Cardinal John Newman in 1997 at San Giorgio in Velabro, Archbishop John Foley preached well on this very point, using as his theme the quote from Newman, "If we wish to be perfect, we have nothing more to do than to perform the ordinary duties of the day well." So, we do our work, fulfill our responsibilities generously and graciously, without notice and complaint. Such is our lot . . . day in and day out, to be the "Cal Ripkens" of the Church, exercising our ministries as followers of Christ reliably with reverence, joy, and zeal. But yet, such daily, unswerving attention to our Christian duty has a penitential dimension.

Has anyone said it better than the Little Flower? She longed for some heroic, dazzling, exotic ministry: Would it be as a missionary in China? Would she be a martyr, perhaps? And then to arrive at that insight so plain and simple that it evades most of us: that the secret of sanctity is to do the ordinary things of life extraordinarily well for the glory of God and love of His people. And that entails what we might call a "passive penance" as daily we pick up our cross and advance a bit with Jesus in His passion and cross.

Is this not the reason we look back with love and admiration upon people who have had a real impact upon our lives, our mothers and fathers, some priests in our lives — nothing dramatic, nothing big sticks out, just day in and day out, reliably being there?

Yes, penance enters our lives as we gracefully embrace the hardships and difficulties that just plain come with life.

St. John of the Cross says: "I saw the river over which every soul must pass to reach the kingdom of heaven, and the name of the river was *suffering* . . . and I saw the boat which carries souls across that river, and the name of that boat was *love*" (emphasis added).

Love and suffering . . . the key words to describe penance, as we are configured to Jesus in His passion and cross so that we may be so in His resurrection. "We carry in our bodies the dying of Jesus," as St. Paul described it.

Let us pray:

We adore Thee, O Christ, and we bless Thee! Because by Thy holy cross Thou hast redeemed the world!

Rejoice in the Lord always; again I will say, Rejoice.
Let all men know your forbearance. The Lord is at
hand. Have no anxiety about anything, but in
everything by prayer and supplication with thanks-
giving let your requests be made known to God.
And the peace of God, which passes all understand-
ing, will keep your hearts and your minds in Christ
Jesus.

— Phil. 4:4–7

CHAPTER 9

—✠—

Joy

*A*s a priest assigned in Washington, D.C., I used to have the privilege of assisting occasionally at the Gift of Peace House, in the northeastern corner of the capital, a hospice for dying AIDS patients conducted by Mother Teresa's Missionaries of Charity. On Good Friday, 1989, I was celebrant of the Liturgy of the Lord's Passion for the sisters, volunteers, and patients. After the assembly had venerated the cross, two sisters led me upstairs so that the bedridden patients could kiss the feet of Our Lord on the cross.

As I went from bed to bed, I noticed one emaciated man in the corner who seemed agitated, and kept beckoning to me to come to him. As I began in turn to approach his bed, the sister halted me, warning that this man was unusually violent, hateful to all, and had actually attempted to bite the attending sisters a number of times. Of course, you realize the consequences of being bitten by one with AIDS. However, the poor man kept signaling for me to come near. What was I to do? What would any priest do? Slowly, cautiously, I approached, and carefully extended the crucifix, which he grasped and kissed — not the feet, I remember so vividly — but the face of the crucified Lord. He then lay back down, exhausted.

The next day, Holy Saturday, the sisters called to tell me that the same man had asked to see me. I went, and, again, in company with two of the sisters as "bodyguards," approached him. As I got nearer he whispered, "I want to be baptized!"

I moved a few inches closer, and, expressing satisfaction, asked if he could explain to me why he desired to enter the Church. "I know nothing about Christianity or the Catholic Church," he said, with the little bit of strength he had left. "In fact, I have hated religion all my life. All I do know is that for three months I have been here dying. These sisters are always happy! When I curse them, they look at me with compassion in their eyes. Even when they clean up my vomit, bathe my sores, and change my diapers, they are smiling; when they spoon-feed me, there is a radiance in their eyes. All I know is that they have joy and I don't. When I ask them in desperation why they are so happy, all they answer is 'Jesus.' I want this Jesus. Baptize me and give me this Jesus! Give me joy!"

Never as a priest has it brought me more satisfaction to baptize, anoint, and give first Holy Communion to someone. He died at 3:15 on Easter morning.

"Joy," wrote the French philosopher Léon Bloy, "is the most infallible sign of God's presence." Faith, hope, love, humility, zeal, penance, fidelity, chastity, penance, and joy — these are all virtues critical in our lives. At first glance, joy might not seem to rank up there too high in the pantheon of Christian virtues, but I exhort you to look again. A Christian without joy is an oxymoron, but, as you well know, "their name is legion," I am afraid.

When I was an assistant at Little Flower Parish back in St. Louis, I met with our parish vocation committee and asked them what we priests and nuns in the parish could do to encourage young people to consider a vocation to the priesthood or religious life. One crusty old guy spoke up, "Well, you can begin by being happy! Show us you love your work and enjoy your life! Be joyful!" Not bad advice.

None other than Andrew Greeley wonders if the major reason for the decline in vocations is simply that we priests and religious have turned into crabs, worried about the future, overwhelmed by work, complaining about everything, fretting about our lives, feeling sorry for ourselves, and taking ourselves way too seriously. Who wants to join an outfit such as that?

I remember being a new student at the North American College in October, 1972, when the cardinal-vicar of Rome, Angelo Dell'Acqua, had the opening Mass for the seminary academic year at St. Peter's Basilica. As he looked out at thousands of priests, sisters, and seminarians, he concluded his homily by saying, "Now I have a favor to ask each of you." We expected some heroic sacrifice or great exhortation to sanctity and scholarship. Instead, he asked, "As you walk the streets of Rome, please smile" — a favor that, those who visit Rome realize, has yet to be granted.

"If the world saw our happiness," wrote St. Madeleine Sophie Barat, "it would, out of sheer envy, invade our churches, houses, and retreats, and the times of the Fathers of the Desert would return when the solitudes were more populous than the cities."

Yes, joy is what most often attracts people to the Church. Catholics are not Puritans. G.K. Chesterton has defined a Puritan as "one who lives in mortal fear that someone somewhere might be having a good time!" I remember once preparing a young couple for marriage; she was Catholic, he was Presbyterian. He at first showed absolutely no interest in the Church, but, after a couple of months, he stopped to see me and told me he wanted to find out more about the Church. "Why?" I inquired, figuring it was some teaching or practice of the Church that may have affected him.

"Well, I've gotten to know Deidre's family so well since we got engaged and, well, they seem to enjoy life, they are so happy." Good Catholics usually are.

Once I was taking a trip through Germany with my first pastor after he had retired. We started in the north of Germany and, by day three, we entered the south, Bavaria. Now, the two of us had gone incognito, and the tour guide had no idea we were priests. As we entered Bavaria, she said, "You'll notice a big change now. Up north, people work hard, there is a lot of industry, the folks are more somber, and life looks drab. Down here, look at the flowers, the painted homes, the chubby, smiling people, lots of kids, good food, dancing, song, and lots of beer." She concluded, "The north is Protestant, the south is Catholic."

Remember G.K. Chesterton's great jingle?

Wherever a Catholic sun doth shine,
There's plenty of laughter and good red wine.
God grant that it be ever so,
Benedicamus Domino!

Now, please keep in mind that, when I say joy, I mean that interior peace about which St. Paul speaks that gives rise to an exterior happiness. I do not mean some giggly, unrealistic, Pollyannaish mania. These people get on your nerves and usually deep down are not at peace. Joy makes us carefree but never careless. A pastor told me about his assistant, a very irresponsible man who laughed a lot, not showing up one Friday morning, meaning the pastor had the two scheduled morning Masses and then the funeral the assistant was supposed to take. When the guy finally showed up, he explained that he had just been carried away by joy out in the countryside and decided to spend the night and enjoy nature. The pastor told him to go back out to the country because he didn't need him around anymore. Genuine joy is realistic, responsible, prudent, deep, and reasonable, not some hollow, empty-headed, childish put-on.

It makes sense that if the Church is joyful, its people had better be people of joy, for, if we are not, we make the "good news" a lie. If we are to be joyful, we'd better find out how to get there.

So, let me ask, where does this joy come from? What is the source of our joy? Of course, joy comes from the Lord, who plants it in the heart of the believer.

Thus, you know that St. Paul lists joy as one of the fruits of the Holy Spirit, a grace, a charism given by God. I could spend a long time giving a list of the ways God is the source of our joy, but let me concentrate on four.

First is the conviction that God loves us. As St. Ignatius recognized in his spiritual exercises, the first step in all growth in holiness is the recognition of God's overwhelming love for me, completely unmerited, totally undeserved. My second-grade teacher taught us to pray every day: "Sacred Heart of Jesus, I place all my trust in thee! / Sacred Heart of Jesus, I believe in your love for me!"

I was in the middle of preparation for this chapter on joy when I came to the Office of Readings for the Tuesday of the third week of Easter, where St. Augustine speaks of Easter joy and its source: we cannot love unless someone has loved us first. Listen to the Apostle John: "We love God because he first loved us." The source of our love for God can only be found in the fact that God loved us first. "The love of God has been poured into our hearts."

"Sacred Heart of Jesus, I believe in your love for me!" That profound conviction that God loves us can cause nothing but joy. Christians are constantly aware of God's infinite love for them, and are eager to convince others of the fact that God loves them as well. To be every moment of our lives fully convinced of God's love for us, to bask in it, to accept it, to express gratitude for it, and to return it in love to God is, of course, the secret of real joy.

A second source of joy flows from this conviction of God's unconditional love for us, namely a belief that He actually dwells within us through the gift of sanctifying grace.

I was a priest for only eight months when I got the toughest convert I've ever had. The parish was holding a mission, and on the third evening a man about my age approached me. He introduced himself as a professor of mathematics from nearby Washington University, and he expressed an interest in Catholicism. Well, for six months I intellectually wrestled with him, going through instructions, knock-down-drag-out fights to all hours of the night during our weekly sessions. Finally, when I completed all the instructions, at our last meeting, he said to me: "You know, there's one point of Catholic teaching I can't accept at all."

"What is it?" I asked, presuming it was going to be one of the regulars, like the Real Presence, the sacrament of penance, the role of Our Lady, or the teaching authority of the pope.

How surprised I was when he went on: "Way back at the beginning, you taught me about something called 'sanctifying grace.' I must have misunderstood you because I thought you explained that sanctifying grace means that the very life of God actually dwells in the soul of the believer, that we literally share in God's life. I obviously misunderstood you, because that would just be too good to be true."

"You understood me perfectly well," I replied. There was a man who fully appreciated the gift of sanctifying grace.

If we not only believe that God loves us passionately, but actually dwells in our soul, you tell me how we can be anything but joyful. To be gratefully aware of God's indwelling then becomes a real source of joy. He will never extinguish that life; only we can do it by mortally offending Him, and then that sanctifying grace can be restored simply for the asking through the sacrament of penance. Thus, the deep joy of a good confession.

That supernatural life, imparted in baptism, must, like natural life, be nourished and cared for, and that is done through prayer, practice of virtue, and the sacraments. A great source of joy is daily worthy reception of the Holy Eucharist. St. Ephrem realized this back in the fourth century when he wrote: "In Your sacrament we daily embrace You and receive You into our hearts; we have had Your treasure hidden within us ever since we received baptismal grace; it grows ever richer at Your sacramental table. Teach us to find *joy* in Your favor."

That we here would have God's own life within us fanned into a flame through our participation in the Eucharist first thing each morning is a genuine blessing, one that would, God willing, be a source of joy all through the day.

So, a second cause of joy is a humble, grateful, awesome, constant awareness of the indwelling of the Trinity, sanctifying grace, deep within our soul. You tell me how we can be mean, spiteful, depressed, if we really believe that at the core of our being God is living with us? As Abbott Marmion wrote, "Joy is the echo of God's life within us."

The third font of joy is a trust, a hope in Divine Providence. If, as is our rock-sure belief, the Lord is omnipotent, all is in His fatherly hands, Jesus has conquered sin, Satan, and death, and, as St. Paul teaches, "in everything God works for good with those who love him," why would sorrow, distress, and setbacks extinguish our joy? The flame may flicker, the winds may threaten to blow it out, but, ultimately, all is in His hands, and all will work out according to His plan. A simple, childlike trust in His Providence gives rise to a joy, a tranquility that no sorrow can dispel.

This is why we are so inspired by the joy often evident in those who, from a human point of view, should be in desperation. Wait until you are struck by the interior joy you detect in the poor and the sick. I suppose it has to be because, without any human resources, they have to exhibit total trust in Divine Providence. As an extraordinary minister of the Eucharist, you might bring Holy Communion to sick people who, in the midst of agonizing pain and infirmity, radiate an interior serenity and happiness. You might also visit people who literally have no idea where their next meal is coming from, but yet are people of joy. And, then, you might come into contact with wealthy, powerful, strong, healthy people who are catty, petty, angry, and unhappy.

Back home in St. Louis, there is a group of physicians who each summer spend two weeks in Haiti. I remember once convincing a pediatrician in our parish to go. He did, and, when he returned, he was beaming. When I asked him what impressed him most, he answered immediately, "The joy of the people! We went into the most destitute conditions I ever saw: mud shacks, families crowded into them, and sick children, and yet the people were happy! They welcomed us and shared with us the little they had. And here, at home," he concluded, "we have so much and seem so sad." Again, that joy has to have its source in a trust in Divine Providence, since they have no one else to hope in.

The final font of joy is prayer. The vocabulary of trust in Divine Providence is, of course, prayer. Think back to our opening passage from Scripture: "By prayer and supplication with thanksgiving let your requests be made known to God."

Now, prayer is a source of joy in two key ways. For one, since, as has been mentioned, joy is a virtue, a charism, a gift from the Lord . . . well, then, if we don't have it or we desire more of it, we ask for it through prayer.

Second, though, the conviction that we can approach God for mercy, help, and direction is a great boost to joy, is it not? That we can give over to God our anxieties and worries removes a serious reason not to be joyful. What do we do with the myriad of naturally valid reasons to be fretting, sullen, and unhappy? We submit them to the Lord in prayer, leaving them to his care, and then, we can be joyful. This seems to be what Charles de Foucauld had in mind when he wrote: "O God, how good you are to allow us to call you 'Our Father.' What gratitude, what joy, what love, and, above all, what confidence this should inspire in me. And as you are my Father and my God, how perfectly I should always hope in you."

Well, as I said, I could expand on sources of joy, but I had better go on to things that can sap our joy. There are many threats to the joy that should exude from Christ's people, you know, and stay with me now as I try to mention a few of them.

A real peril to joy is self-pity. People today can swim in self-pity, especially with all the crises around us. Self-pity hardly causes joy. That's when we get grumpy, listless, and burdened. Poor me! Of course, the problem is that the "me" becomes the focus, I become the center of my thought and energy instead of Jesus and the people He places in my path. Put Jesus first, then others, then yourself, and therein is joy. Self-pity, of course, inverts that and puts the self first.

A second temptation to joy is worry. Lord knows there's plenty to worry about. Our worries can preoccupy us and turn us inward, taking the joy out of our lives.

I remember a woman telling me she considered worry a sin. Never having heard that before, I asked her to explain. "Well," she replied, "I figure I sin against faith if I worry too much. Jesus told us not to be anxious, not to worry, that our heavenly Father knows what we need and will take care of us. When I worry, I am not trusting his promise." What a wise woman she was! Worry is a sin against faith, and can destroy joy. So you see people who just act like they have the weight of the world on their shoulders. They can't take any time off, they can't relax, they can't go on retreat, because there are just so many things to get done and, of course, it all depends on me!

Remember the pastor I mentioned earlier, who wouldn't take vacations? When he would finally go away for a week, he would usually come back early, frantically ask how everything had gone in his absence, and almost get mad that everything had gone so well. Yes, cemeteries are filled with people who believed the world could not go on without them. We fret and worry that all depends on us, mostly because we want it to and need that control. But can that kind of worry ever take a toll on joy!

I know I have some worriers reading this: money, work, problems at home — we can find dozens of reasons to worry. But, as Jesus said, it won't add one cubit to our span of existence. And when we worry too much, we see other people as a nuisance and a bother; thus, we hardly exude joy.

A third threat to joy is the heresy that our happiness depends upon something outside of ourselves. Thus, we lose joy if we feel we were passed over for a position we wanted; we become sullen if the boss says no to a particular project or request we had . . .

Joy does not depend on acclaim, advancement, promotion, recognition, fame, prestige, or power. Joy can never come from without — it can only come from the Lord, who plants it deep inside. If our joy is contingent upon affirmation, success, or career, it is planted in sand and will never endure.

Actually, our joy should have nothing to do with where we work, what we're doing, or any external reward or recognition we get. It only depends on who we are, not what we do or have. We are beloved of the Father, configured to His Son, alive with His grace, sealed with His promise — everything else is gravy. If we're counting on anything or anyone outside of the Lord to cause our joy, we're setting ourselves up for a fall. The saddest people are those who longed for titles, acclaim, and advancement, and never got them, or those who got them and then realized they still lacked joy. Oh, yes, those things may bring pleasure, but, remember, pleasure is not joy! As C. S. Lewis says in his masterpiece on joy: "Joy is never in our power, and pleasure is. I doubt whether anyone who has tasted joy would ever, if both were in his power, exchange it for all the pleasure in the world."

A fourth danger to joy is complaining. We can really be like children when it comes to griping. I once heard Archbishop John May say, "Some guys would have complained about the menu at the Last Supper." You will quickly discover that there are two kinds of people: those who work hard, try their best, are not afraid of risk or failure, and then those who sit back and complain, pointing out how it should have been done. In other words, you've got those who play hard on the field, and then the others who criticize on the sidelines. I hope to God you are among the first group. If you, please God, are in the first group, be prepared for carping and petty complaints from group two.

"Joy is the infallible sign of God's presence." I conclude by turning to the "Cause of Our Joy":

Mother benign of our redeeming Lord,
Star of the Sea and portal of the skies,
Unto your fallen people help afford —
Fallen, but striving still anew to rise.
You who once while wondering worlds adored,
Bore your Creator, Virgin then as now,
O by your holy joy at Gabriel's word,
Pity the sinners who now before you bow.

In the days of his flesh, Jesus offered up prayers and supplications, with loud cries and tears, to him who was able to save him from death, and he was heard for his godly fear. Although he was a Son, he learned obedience through what he suffered; and being made perfect he became the source of eternal salvation to all who obey him, being designated by God a high priest after the order of Melchizedek.

— HEB. 5:7–10

CHAPTER 10

Obedience

"Jf today you hear his voice, harden not your hearts," could be the most frequent verse in the divine office, since we repeat it seven times each week during the Invitatory, Psalm 95. Wise mother she is, the Church knows we need that daily exhortation to live the virtue of obedience.

Obedience could be the easiest virtue to describe, but the toughest to live. Obedience is simply conforming our lives to the will of God, submitting ourselves to His dominion as expressed in the Bible, in the Tradition and magisterium of the Church, in natural law, in the directives of our legitimate superiors, in the dictates of a well-formed conscience, and in the prompting of the Holy Spirit interpreted prudently in discernment.

So basic is it that it was the only virtue expected of our first parents, and the Creator's gracious design was tragically distorted by that "original sin" which was an act of willful, proud disobedience. As the French philosopher Michel de Montaigne observed:

> The first law that ever God gave to man was a law of obedience. It was a commandment pure and simple, wherein man had nothing to inquire after or to dispute, for as much as to obey is the proper office of a rational soul acknowledging a heavenly superior and benefactor. From obedience and submission spring all the other virtues, as all sin does from self-opinion and self-will.

Thus is the generous act of obedience by Our Lady at the Annunciation seen as the "right" wherein the primordial "wrong" of the first Eve is corrected by the second. As Irenaeus remarked, "The seduction of a fallen angel drew Eve, while the glad tidings of the holy angel drew Mary, to begin the plan which would dissolve the bonds of the first snare.... So the Virgin Mary has become the advocate for the Virgin Eve.... Life has triumphed by the Virgin Mary's obedience, which has finally balanced the debt of disobedience."

Thus is Jesus extolled as the perfectly obedient Son. "Thirty years of Our Lord's life are hidden in these words of the Gospel: 'He was subject unto them,'" preached the French bishop Jacques Bossuet. However, this is even more evident in his embrace of the cross — as tragic, illogical, desperate, useless, and spiteful as pride might interpret it — that Jesus was most obedient. "For Christ became obedient, even unto death, death on a cross." Irenaeus again: "In the first Adam we offended God by not performing his command. In the second Adam we have been reconciled, becoming 'obedient unto death.'"

However, as much as we recognize its pivotal importance, obedience is one of the most difficult virtues to practice, because it goes against a power that makes the neutron bomb look like a Bic lighter: the stubborn, proud human will.

"...Obedience! / Bane of all genius, virtue, freedom, and truth / makes slaves of men, and of the human frame / a mechanized automaton...," muses the poet Shelley in what has to be the common understanding of obedience.

My own spiritual director believes that it is precisely in obedience — not in celibacy, strangely enough — that the priest of today is most countercultural. For we live in a world that divinizes the will, holding that true happiness only comes when you have the license to do what you want, when you want, with whom and to whom you want, how you want, where you want; and that any restraint based on obedience to any higher authority is unjust, oppressive, and to be defied — since, as a matter of fact, there is no "higher authority" than my own wants, needs, and will.

This culture of denigrating obedience is particularly obvious in our beloved United States of America, which was founded on disobedience. We legitimately celebrate the courageous patriotism of the revolutionaries who risked all to gain independence from an oppressive king, yes, but we also admit that at times we tend to equate liberty with license, freedom with rights unbridled by duty; that we exalt dissent over docility, and view with suspicion authority, tradition, and acceptance of things purely on faith. Those familiar with the history of the Church in America know that a major reason for the ingrained anti-Catholicism of American society is the stereotype that Catholics are mindless, shackled peons who are required to give blind obedience to a corrupt, medieval, foreign system. We grudgingly admire the shrewd public-relations coup of the pro-abortion lobby that has so effectively used the "pro-choice" label, pandering to this American resistance to the thought of "anyone forcing me to do anything." Astute foreign observers of the American scene, from Tocqueville to Solzhenitsyn, and from Bedini to Mother Teresa, have keenly perceived this flaw in American society: namely to resist obedience to God, to tradition, and to moral principles for the sake of choice, convenience, or personal preference. Recent emphasis on self-fulfillment, self-actualization, taking care of oneself — all legitimate goods, by the way, when properly understood — has only deepened this American suspicion of obedience.

So my spiritual director's hunch is probably correct: in a society that urges us to keep all options open, not to be tied down, always to be ready to move on to something more attractive, to place conditions on all pledges, to protect our own interests above all else, to move up and make more, to demand rights and resist restrictions — priests pledge complete obedience to one man and one confined area of God's vineyard. That's countercultural!

And, of course, the paradox comes because all Christians who are obedient to God are evidence of the deeper truth: that it is precisely in obedience that the fullest freedom comes, that lasting peace is attained only when we are led not by our will but by his.

When I was newly ordained, there was a fine woman religious as principal of our grade school. She was one of the youngest and most talented in her order, and I worried about her because her congregation was collapsing, regrouping, closing apostolates, and in seeming disarray. I once asked her, "What will your future hold?" I never forgot her answer.

"I don't know and I don't really care. How freeing it is not to have to worry about my future. That's the gift of obedience."

Thus the paradox: the most liberated people are those most under obedience. The martyrs of the city of Rome by their example converted thousands who came to watch them die, expecting to see frightened, shackled, and depressed slaves forced to their deaths, but instead saw courageous, confident, free, joyful men and women more liberated than their persecutors, people whose obedience to God freed them from all earthly trepidation, compromise, or doubt. Is this not what St. Thérèse of Lisieux had in mind when she wrote her Carmelite superior: "Isn't it extraordinary what a lot of nervous strain you can avoid by taking the vow of obedience? How enviable it is, the simple creed of the religious, who has only one compass to steer by, the will of her superior? She knows for certain that she is on the right path."

Or, as St. Philip Neri observed, "Entire conformity to the divine will is truly a road on which we cannot go wrong, and it is the only road that leads us to taste and enjoy the peace which sensual and earthly men know nothing of."

Can we take a look in more detail at obedience, and begin by considering it in the broadest sense: obedience as listening to God? How many times have you heard in a homily that "to obey" and "to hear" come from the same Latin root? So, let's examine this obedience to God for a few moments.

I recall once meeting with a seminarian when I was spiritual director back at Kenrick Seminary in St. Louis. In response to his forthright expression of quandary over his priestly vocation, I launched into a glib exposé on the necessity of obeying God's will.

"Father," he pleaded, "my problem is not obeying God's will; my problem is finding out what it is!" How very true! When God's will is clear, it might take sacrifice to obey it, but at least we know what we should do. The problem comes when His will is not clear. Then what?

The process of discovering God's will is called discernment, and it is a noble and sacred enterprise. One phenomenon essential to discerning God's will and then obeying it is prayer. If obedience is predicated upon listening to God, then we had better listen hard, and that comes in prayer.

We cannot be obedient disciples unless we ensure that there is a period of prayer every day, and one of our major duties in life is to develop the habit of prayer. We cannot know God's will unless we pray.

The legendary president of Notre Dame, Father Theodore Hesburgh, remarks in his autobiography that the achievements of his life could never have happened "without inner peace, born of prayer, especially to the Holy Spirit, in search of light, inspiration, and courage. I have a simple three-word prayer that has served me well for many, many years: 'Come, Holy Spirit.' It has never failed me."

But I have a particular form of prayer in mind, essential to this listening to the Lord and at the core of obedience. Most of us would get a "B" or above when it comes to a more active type of prayer: daily Mass, the divine office, our rosary, spiritual reading, devotions, quick visits to the Blessed Sacrament, and favorite prayers. Not to take away from the importance of this more "active" prayer, but I'm afraid most of us hover around a "D" when it comes to that more passive kind of prayer where we do nothing but open ourselves to Our Lord's movements. That's meditation; that's contemplation; that's hard. To listen to the voice of the Lord, to sense His presence, to absorb His love, grace, and mercy . . . that's when we listen so we can obey.

We'd rather talk, wouldn't we?

I am reminded of the story of the father who died, leaving behind a grieving wife and two sons. The one son was not home when his dad died and rushed back, went right to his brother, who had been at the bedside when his dad had expired, and asked, "Tell me how dad died. Did he have any last words?"

To which the other son said, "No, dad had no last words. Mom was there with him till the end."

That's us: so busy talking, telling God what we want, telling Him how to be God, that we miss His subtle whispers. "The value of persistent prayer is not that God will hear us, but that we will finally hear God," writes William McGill. This quiet, patient, calm, passive, listening prayer is hard, slow, and painful work. But keep at it we must. We cannot discern His will, much less obey it, unless we keep at it.

"If today you hear his voice, harden not your hearts!" Obedience to God.

A monk at the Abbey of Gethsemani told me how he was happy with his work in the bakery when one day the abbot told him he wanted him to be ordained a priest. After his years of preparation, he was ordained and, the day after his first Mass, waited for the abbot after morning prayer to ask what his new assignment would be. The abbot was surprised and said, "Why, return to the bakery, of course."

"But," the young monk replied, "that's what I did before I was ordained."

"Yes, but now you'll do it as a priest," replied the abbot.

It was precisely at the lowest point of His earthly life, at the time He felt most abandoned, most forgotten, the most useless, the time He hurt the most — at the time of greatest suffering — on the cross, obedient even unto death, that Jesus accomplished the most.

If the goal of our lives is conformity to Christ, then obedience is the path to get there. St. Ignatius of Loyola taught:

> Obedience is a whole burnt offering in which the entire man, without the slightest reserve, is offered in the fire of charity to his Creator and Lord. . . . Few souls understand what God would accomplish in them if they were to abandon themselves unreservedly to him, and if they were to allow his grace to mold them accordingly.

St. John Vianney, who himself was tempted often to leave Ars for other easier assignments, but who each time accepted the bishop's will, preached, "Obedience makes the will supple. It gives the power to conquer self, to overcome laziness, and to resist temptations. It inspires the courage with which to fulfill the most difficult tasks."

Obedience then is that mediating virtue through which all the others come; we pursue holiness, humility, chastity, simplicity, and charity because we are attentive to God's will, obedient to His designs, and we know this is what He wants. He has a plan for us, and we cooperate. It is rarely clear as we anticipate it in the future; it usually is as we reflect upon it looking back, if we have been obedient.

As we find in Cardinal John Newman's meditations:

> God has created me to do him some definite service; he has committed some work to me which he has not committed to another. I have my mission — I may never know it in this life, but I shall be told it in the next.
>
> He has not created me for nothing. I shall do good, I shall do his work, I shall be an angel of peace, a preacher of the truth in my own place — if I do but keep his commandments and serve him in my calling.
>
> Therefore, I will trust him. Whatever, wherever I am, I can never be thrown away. If I am in sickness, my sickness may serve him; if I am in sorrow, my sorrow may serve him.
>
> He does nothing in vain. He knows what he is about. He may take away my friends. He may throw me among strangers. He may make me feel desolate, make my spirits sink, hide my future from me — still he knows what he is about — and I trust him.

So, in our obedience to God we are most in conformity to Jesus, placing our plans, our desires, and our wills at the disposal of the Father. We close with the *Suscipe* of Charles de Foucauld:

Father,
>I abandon myself into your hands;
>do with me what you will.
>Whatever you may do, I thank you:
>I am ready for all, I accept all.
>Let only your will be done in me,
>and in all your creatures —
>I wish no more than this, O Lord.
>Into your hands I commend my soul;
>I offer it to you
>with all the love of my heart,
>for I love you, Lord,
>and so need to give myself,
>to surrender myself
>into your hands,
>without reserve,
>and with boundless confidence,
>for you are my Father.

Then they returned to Jerusalem from the mount called Olivet, which is near Jerusalem, a sabbath day's journey away; and when they had entered, they went up to the upper room, where they were staying, Peter and John and James and Andrew, Philip and Thomas, Bartholomew and Matthew, James the son of Alphaeus and Simon the Zealot and Judas the son of James. All these with one accord devoted themselves to prayer, together with the women and Mary the mother of Jesus, and with his brothers.

— Acts 1:12–14

CHAPTER 11

---†---

Devotion to Our Lady

When I was rector there, nine times out of ten I sat on the pulpit side of the sanctuary for morning prayer and Mass in our chapel at the North American College. The reason I did so was simple. At that time of the day, I needed all the help I could get in concentrating and focusing. From that side I could look straight at the mural of the Annunciation that dominates the opposite wall, and, for me, that early concentration on Mary and the Archangel Gabriel supplied the "first aid," the focus I needed. According to art scholar Kenneth Clark, the Annunciation is the most re-created scene in the history of painting, so apparently I am not alone in finding it magnetic.

When I asked three of our students who had just returned from the Holy Land what place most moved them during their pilgrimage, they each replied separately, "The Church of the Annunciation in Nazareth;" specifically, the seal in the floor, *Hic Verbum caro factum est* ("Here the Word was made Flesh").

So, again, I find myself in good company being attracted by the Annunciation. "The Annunciation," wrote Martin Luther, "when the angel came to Mary and brought her the message from God, may be fitly called the Feast of Christ's humanity, for then began our deliverance."

The angel of the Lord announced unto Mary.
And she conceived by the Holy Spirit.
Behold the handmaid of the Lord.

Be it done unto me according to Thy Word.
And the Word became flesh.
And dwelt among us.

This is the Incarnation, the pivotal mystery of Christianity; the "good news" — that God became man, the Word became flesh, the second Person of the Blessed Trinity took upon himself human nature in the womb of a virgin. It is that truth that provides me a focus each morning, it is that scene of the Virgin that reminds me, as I start the day, of my identity, my vocation, my mission.

For, as Bishop Fulton Sheen has so eloquently preached, the real good news is that the Incarnation continues, as the Word of God is enfleshed each day in the heart and mind, speech and actions, of His disciples. So does every follower of Christ identify closely with Mary, for the fundamental question posed to them, the answer to which gives them identity, and mission is the same one posed to her at the Annunciation: Will you give flesh to the Son of God? Will the divine become human through you? Will you provide God the Son with a human nature? As I would sit in one of those chairs and look at Mary, my mission, identity, and vocation as a priest was reaffirmed. I was reminded that in a matter of minutes, at the altar, I would sacramentally provide God flesh, and I resolved that throughout the day, with his help, the Lord would become again incarnate for His people in and through me.

Rome, the Eternal City, fosters a love of Mary. From the ancient frescoes at the catacombs to St. Mary Major and Santa Maria in Trastevere; from the *Salus Populi Romani* to Our Lady of Perpetual Help at St. Alphonsus; from the charming parochial and neighborhood feasts to her image that adorns almost every *angolo* ("corner") of this city — she is there.

And then, of course, there is the powerful example of the
Bishop of Rome, who, probably more than anyone, is responsible for the current renaissance in Marian piety. His manly, genuine, evangelical love of her has animated every address,
encyclical, word, travel, and pastoral initiative of his extraordinary pontificate. His conclusion to *Gift and Mystery* could well
serve as a commentary on his whole pastorate:

> May the Virgin Mary accept this testimony of mine as
> a filial homage, for the glory of the Blessed Trinity. May
> she make it fruitful in the hearts of my brothers in the
> priesthood and of all the members of the Church. May she
> make it a leaven of solidarity for the many good people
> who, although they do not share the same faith, often lis-
> ten to my words and engage me in sincere dialogue.

We can testify that this hope of the Holy Father has certainly been fulfilled.

The Church — in fact, the world — is experiencing a
tremendous renewal of attention and dedication to Mary. *Life*
magazine had her on its cover in their December, 1996 issue. In
a well-done article they tried to discover what they termed "the
mystery of Mary," concluding that attraction to her is one of the
world's most potent forces, luring not only Catholics and the
Orthodox as it always has, but Muslims, Protestants, Jews, and
people of no creed whatever.

Allow the historian in me to take over for a minute to
observe that, within recent memory of many, devotion to Mary
was not always as popular as it is now. In the heady, difficult,
cleansing years after the providential Second Vatican Council,
many felt the Reformation discomfort with her had finally
reached even Rome, and that she had been at last relegated to

the storage rooms and museums. There were calls for a more rational, calm, theologically proper, cerebral attention to Mary. Some even began to ridicule Marian piety. As I will explain shortly, perhaps some of this reform was necessary and even beneficial, but we do know now that a tender love of the Mother of Jesus is so strong and so ingrained in the Christian psyche that it could not be erased. As Cardinal Carlo Martini recently commented in Milan: "I believe the time has come to take a new look at Marian devotion, to find an equilibrium between theological clarity and the spiritual yearnings of the Christian people. Otherwise, we may face a dangerous loss of warmth and feeling in our faith, our prayer, our life. . . . We have arrived at a point where this cold, scientific attitude no longer responds to an obvious emotional need for an attachment to Mary."

So just as there were unfortunate excesses in the postconciliar renewal of Marian devotion, there were excesses in the piety itself prior to the council. I hope I am not being naïve in agreeing with the archbishop of Milan that perhaps now, having seen extremes on both sides, we can benefit from the renewed, sound devotion to Our Lady that seems to be sweeping the Church today.

A valuable catechesis in genuine love of Our Lady came from Pope Paul VI in his apostolic letter of 1974, *Marialis Cultis*, on the right ordering of veneration to Mary. Rejecting both the saccharine, overly sentimental, and doctrinally questionable devotion to her that characterized some circles prior to the council and the dry, rationalistic downplaying of her central role indicative of some in the late sixties and the seventies, Paul VI called for a genuine, reinvigorated veneration to Mary; a *cultus* purified of any taint of so-called Mariolatry, but emphatic about her indispensable role in the economy of salvation.

He proposed four checks to make sure our devotion to the Mother of God was pure, sound, and mature: that it be Christological, scriptural, liturgical and ecclesial, and ecumenically sensitive. I submit these are worth reviewing now in our ongoing desire to ensure that our devotion to the Blessed Mother is with the Church.

Veneration of Mary is *Christological* as we observe the old maxim that goes *"Ad Jesum per Mariam"* ("To Jesus through Mary"). The only goal of attention to Mary, as it is the only goal of anything we do, is to reach Jesus. It is simple Catholic wisdom that one of the more effective, reliable, enjoyable, and tender ways of growing closer to Jesus is by holding the hand of His Mother. The woman whose last recorded words in the Gospel are, "Do whatever he tells you," resists and disdains more than anyone else any attempt to place her above or in front of her Son.

Can there ever be an excess of Marian piety? Well, there can certainly be an excess of wrong Marian piety! However, there can hardly ever be an overabundance of genuine, properly ordered devotion to her. As St. Bernard preached, "Let us not imagine that we obscure the glory of the Son by the honor we lavish on the Mother, for the more she is honored, the greater is the glory of her Son." Listen to Pope John Paul describe his early veneration of Mary in his memoir, *Gift and Mystery*:

> At the time when my priestly vocation was developing ... a change took place in my understanding of devotion to the Mother of God. I was already convinced that Mary leads us to Christ, but at that time I began to realize also that Christ leads us to his Mother. At one point I began to question my devotion to Mary, believing that, if it became too great, it might end up compromising the supremacy of the worship owed to Christ. At that time I was greatly helped by a book by St. Louis Marie Grignion de Montfort, *Treatise of True Devotion to the Blessed Virgin*.

There I found the answers to my questions. Yes, Mary does bring us closer to Christ; she does lead us to him, provided we live her mystery in Christ. . . . This is the origin of the motto *Totus Tuus,* an abbreviation of the more complete form of entrustment which reads: *Totus tuus ego sum et omnia mea Tua sunt. Accipio Te in mea omnia. Praebe mihi cor Tuum, Maria.* (I belong to you entirely, and all that I possess is yours. I take you into everything that is mine. Give me your heart, O Mary.)

If our attention to Mary stops with her, it is wrong. She loves being a means to an end, the end being her Son. True, genuine, orthodox veneration of Mary is always Christological.

Likewise it is *scriptural,* says Pope Paul VI. All we need for a rich, sustaining Marian piety is found in the Bible. This does not mean that the Church's tantalizing array of feasts, titles, apparitions, prayers, songs, poetry, and traditions are misguided. No, they are so welcome and helpful because they flow from, enhance, and enliven God's revelation about His chosen daughter contained in Scripture, passed on in Tradition, and guarded by the magisterium. A pure and genuine devotion to her is not dependent upon the more exotic features of apparitions, secrets, miracles, and new revelations. Thomas Merton said it well: "Since God has revealed very little to us about Mary, people who know nothing of who and what she was only reveal themselves when they try to add something to what God has already told us about her."

Thus, genuine veneration of Mary is Scripture-based.

It is also *liturgical and ecclesial.* The richest way the Church honors Mary is in the Church's official public prayer, celebrating her feasts and content with the liturgical prayers we are blessed with. Again, private devotions and prayers are laudable, as long as they flow from and lead us to the corporate praise of the Church, the liturgy. The term used by Pope Paul is ecclesial, for we are wary of an excessively individualistic Marian devotion. Finally, says Pope Paul VI, we should be mindful of the *ecumenical* dimensions of our attention to Mary. Positively, this means we are eager to share with our separated brethren the richness of true devotion to her. Negatively, this means we are sensitive about reformed and evangelical uneasiness caused by past errors and excesses.

By the way, a most welcome ecumenical development you may already know about is that reformed and evangelical Christians are slowly gaining an appreciation of Mary's role. You may have seen one of the most powerful contemporary studies on her: the work of the great Lutheran scholar Jaroslav Pelikan, *Mary Through the Centuries.* I remember a few years ago after the terrible TWA flight 800 tragedy hearing Dr. Forrest Church, pastor of the Unitarian All Souls Church in New York, remark: "People were asking, 'How can God allow such a thing?' But then they'd turn around and pray for the victims, and I watched many pray to Mary ... for support and nurturing. And I mean nurturing in a strong, not a weak way. She would put their tough questions to God on their behalf! She would lift them up and help them move forward! I envy Catholicism its Mary."

Yes, you heard me! This from a Unitarian!

So, a genuine devotion to her is Christological, scriptural, liturgical and ecclesial, and ecumenically mature.

It goes without saying that the most obvious way Mary helps us is through her intercession. "There is no more excellent way to obtain graces from God," concludes St. Philip Neri, "than to seek them through Mary, because her divine Son cannot refuse her anything."

We can never go wrong in turning to her, as did her Son. Especially in trial, temptation, and loneliness can we find in her an attentive ear and a soft shoulder — and, believe me, I know that from experience. You will find that those who struggle with chastity, temperance, doubt, despair, and illness have a very warm and intimate relationship with her. So, most obviously, she helps us because she is a powerful intercessor. The Curé of Ars preached, "It is enough to turn to Mary to be heard. 'My Mother,' Our Lord said to her, 'I cannot refuse you anything.' "

One of my best friends as a priest was very close to his mother, especially after the death of his father. After the passing of her husband, his mother had struggled with bouts of depression, and even had to be hospitalized. It was so moving to watch my friend so lovingly care for her. On one of his days off, he showed up at home to spend the day with her, only to discover that she had taken her own life. You can imagine his devastation.

A few weeks after the funeral, he went through with the plans he had made a year before and came here to Rome for the international retreat for priests. He was at a real low point in his life. Never had he felt so alone, so orphaned. A turning point, he tells me, came during a prayer service in the Audience Hall when an icon of the Mother and Child was carried in. At that moment, gazing at the icon, surrounded by thousands of his brother priests in prayer, he realized that Mary was truly his Mother. He joined her at the foot of the cross. He broke down in tears, and two of the priests near him took him outside and listened as he told them the tragedy of his mother's suicide and his own discovery of Mary just moments before in the prayer service. He marks that episode as the beginning of spiritual rebirth for him.

Thus is she there for everyone.

But I contend that she can also assist us by her example. Specifically, she teaches us, as no other person can, about the earthiness of the Church.

"Mary is our only savior from an abstract Christ," observes the English poet and critic Coventry Patmore. The God who was conceived and carried in her womb, born in a stable, nursed at her breasts, cried on her shoulder, and grew under her care, can hardly be abstract and unreal. Neither He — nor His Mystical Body, the Church — is always neat, tidy, predictable, and clean.

I've quoted before what Walker Percy wrote to the novelist Mary Lee Settle when she became a Catholic, "It's a very untidy outfit you're hooking up with." As a priest told me once when I was in the seminary, "If you want it all nice, clean, presentable, and neat, join the Anglicans." Nothing comfortable and cozy about any of this — it can be messy, untidy, earthy — all synonyms for "incarnational," and woe to those who forget that.

Mary teaches us that discipleship, serving her Son, brings uncertainty. (Sometimes I wonder if, about the time of the flight into Egypt, Mary was ready to get in touch with Gabriel and call it all off.) We can become proud of résumés and have a career path all charted out. Instead, Our Lady smiles and says that when you say *fiat* to the Lord you are surrendering your most prized commodity — your future and your security to plan your life. Get ready for surprises, some plums, some prunes, some Bethlehems, some lost-in-the-temple episodes. In other words, be prepared for uncertainty.

Our Blessed Mother shows us the necessity of fidelity in both the joys and the sorrows of discipleship. She was there at the happiest moment ever — the first Christmas. And she was there at the saddest place ever — the foot of the cross. Likewise will our lives have their Bethlehems and their Calvarys. Her lesson is that what is happening to us is not as significant as with whom it is happening; what is of the essence is that, at both the crib and the cross, she is close to Jesus. That is fidelity.

Mary's impact would be much less had we only the account of her at Christmas and not at Calvary, had we only the Madonna with Child and not the Pietà. So are we faithful to the Church when it is fresh, full of life and promise, alive and bouncy — as was the Infant of Bethlehem; and we are faithful to Christ and his Church when it is dead, lifeless, bleeding and torn — as on Calvary.

An old saying goes, "God may not have favorites, but his Mother does." Our Lady exemplifies a special care for certain people, namely the sick, forgotten, poor, sinful, and troubled. We call her "comforter of the afflicted," "refuge of sinners," "health of the sick," "help of Christians." As a good mother will display a special love for whichever of her children might be sick, troubled, or ignored by the others, so does Mary for her spiritual children. Go to Lourdes, for instance: do not expect to find the wealthy, the strong, the sleek, or the elite, but watch the twisted, battered, tired, and sick in mind, soul, and body bask in a mother's care.

Our Lady teaches us to show a special concern to those in need; they — the sick, poor, the sinners, and the troubled — are her favorites, as they should be ours.

I was inspired by the recent example of Father Juan Julio Wicht, the priest in Lima, Peru, who was one of the hostages in the Japanese Embassy a few years ago. The terrorists wanted to let him go; they told him he was free to leave whenever he wanted. He did not; he chose to stay with the people, to support them, comfort them, pray with and for them. Now there's a great priest, knowing his vocation is to be close to people who need him.

Mary can teach us a dignity and respect for women. Strong and confident, she has a pivotal role in God's plan. God honored her more than any human being, and, in so doing, as Pope John

Paul II reminds us in his apostolic letter *Mulieris Dignitatem*, put to rest the notion that women are inferior and have fewer rights than men. The English critic, essayist, and reformer John Ruskin observes, "There has probably not been an innocent home throughout Europe during the period of Christianity in which the imagined presence of the Madonna has not given sanctity to the duties and comfort to the trials and the lives of women."

You see, any religion which holds that the second Person of the Blessed Trinity took flesh in the womb of a woman, that God himself waited upon the free consent of a woman before proceeding with his plans, that the only human person in heaven, body and soul, is a woman, then that religion, that Church, knows the dignity of women, a true feminism, and that Church is a defender of women's rights in their most elementary sense. Comments Jaroslav Pelikan on the Annunciation, "The entire plan of salvation hung in the balance. So if God does not rape, God woos, then it had to be a free and independent source of action in Mary that made this happen. This makes her not just some passive receptacle."

And as the novelist Mary Gordon mentions, "Devotion to Mary is the objective correlative of all the primitive desires that lead human beings to the life of faith. She embodies our desire to be fully human yet to transcend death. The hatred of women is the legacy of death; in Mary, Mother and Queen, we see, enfleshed in a human form that touches our most ancient longings, the promise of salvation. . . ."

You want a model of how to treat women? Look at how God treated Mary.

One final way Our Lady helps us is by reminding us of our identity.

The author-psychologist Robert Coles has observed that usually the first moment of self-identity a baby has is when the infant, held up by its mother, stares into its mother's eyes and sees there its own reflection. For the first time ever, in the eyes of its mom, the baby realizes it is someone different, that it has an identity.

May I propose that an effective way we Christians discover our identity is by gazing into the eyes of our Blessed Mother? Therein we see the reflection of Jesus, and therein we see ourselves.

She literally carried the Word-made-flesh inside her. She sensed the movement, growth, and life of the God-man within her. So must we imitate her in allowing Jesus to move, grow, and come to life within us. Such is our identity as Christians.

In June 1996, I visited the Shrine of Our Lady of Guadalupe. Reading up on it beforehand, I was fascinated by the story of Mary's eyes. Under scientific, microscopic examination of the *tilma* on which, as you know, the image of Mary was imprinted, the scholars had discovered that in the eyes of the Virgin they detected a reflection of another person, and that person fit the description of Juan Diego.

The day I went to the shrine was a time of pilgrimage for priests. I stood on the platform in front of Mary's image observing, praying, and watching as hundreds of priests, old and young, sick and strong, white, brown, and black, processed in front of her, looking into her eyes. And I imagined the reflection of each individual person in the eyes of the Virgin, as she looks at each one of us with the same intensity, passion, and motherly love as she did Jesus, as she did Juan Diego. She helps us discover, deepen, and persevere in our identity, our vocation, and our mission.

Vergine Immacolata! Aiutateci!
("Immaculate Virgin! Help us!")

Afterword

*S*anctity," claims St. Maximilian Kolbe, "is not a luxury for the few . . . it is a simple duty for us all."

Shortly after I arrived in the Archdiocese of Milwaukee as archbishop, a reporter asked me, "So, Archbishop, you wanted to be a priest, and you were; then you got to be a monsignor; then, just a year ago, a bishop; now you are an archbishop. What's your goal now? To be a cardinal?"

"Actually," I replied, "my goal is to be a saint . . . and to help you be one, too!"

I sure hope this book helps us both achieve that end.